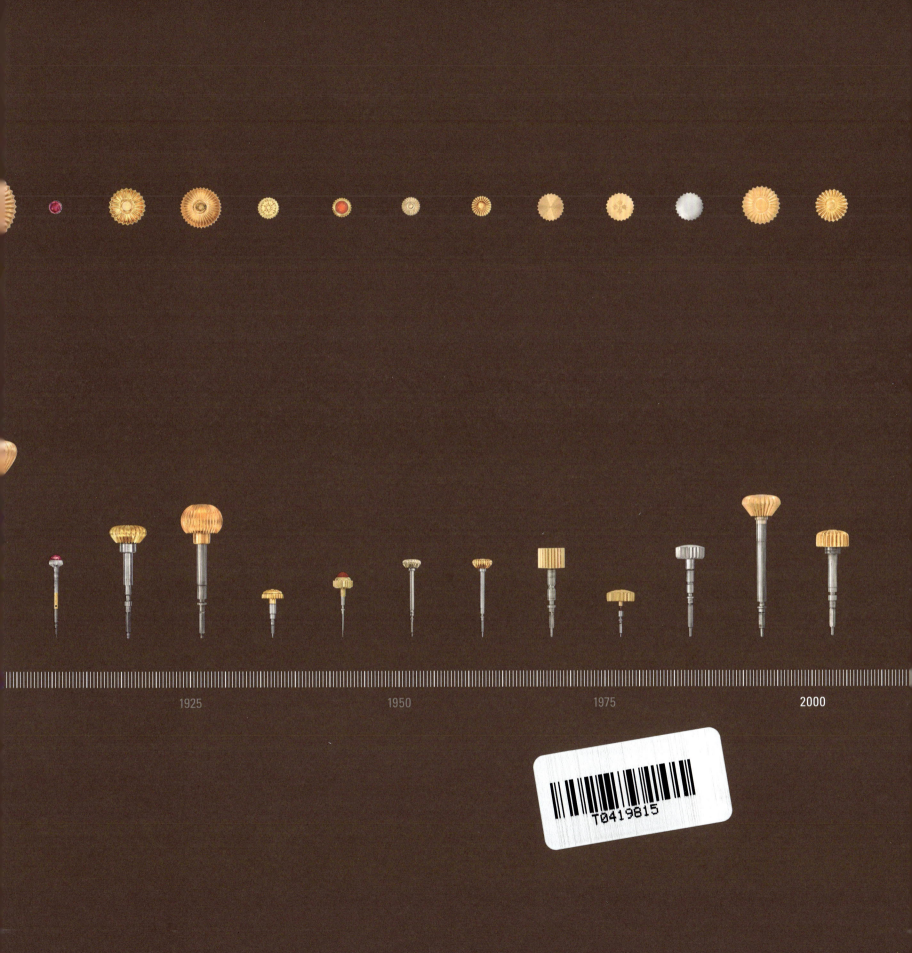

PATEK PHILIPPE MUSEUM

Treasures from The Patek Philippe Collection
The Quest for the Perfect Watch

1800   1850   1900   1950   2000

Peter Friess

PATEK PHILIPPE MUSEUM

Treasures from The Patek Philippe Collection
The Quest for the Perfect Watch

1800　　　1850　　　1900　　　1950　　　2000

2022

Author
Peter Friess, Director and Curator
Patek Philippe Museum

Concept and Design
Birgit Binner, tg2b

Scientific Editing
Arthur Molella

Photography
Photo Studio Fabien Cruchon
Graziano Villa, page 7

Image Retouching
Oeil Absolu Sàrl

Paper and Font
Finesse Premium Silk 170 g/sqm, UPM
Univers, Linotype

Published by teNeues Publishing Group
www.teneues.com

© 2022 Patek Philippe Museum
Any reproduction must be approved by
Patek Philippe SA

Patek Philippe Museum
Rue des Vieux-Grenadiers 7
CH-1205 Genève
www.patekmuseum.com
info@patekmuseum.com

Deutsche Nationalbibliothek
dnb.dnb.de

Library of Congress Control Number
2022935379

ISBN
978-3-96171-397-4

Preface by Philippe Stern		6
Honorary President, Patek Philippe SA		
Precision and Beauty		

Patek Philippe | 8
1839 onwards
Quest for the Perfect Watch

Era of the Industrial Revolution | 10
1839–1851
Origins of the Company

Rhythms of Progress | 14
1851–1894
The Power of a Key(less) Invention

On the World Stage | 20
1851 onwards
Going to the Fairs

In Pursuit of Precision | 24
1873–1968
Chronometers and Observatory Trials

Innovations in Marketing | 30
1872–1936
Exporting to South America

Tracking Time Eternal | 34
1861 onwards
Perpetual Calendars

Embracing Modernism | 38
1890–1932
Art Nouveau and Art Deco

Jumping Forward in Time | 44
1840–1913
One of Jean Adrien Philippe's Last Patents

Chasing Time Around a Faster World | 46
1937 onwards
World Time Watches

Paradox of Modernity | 50
1839 onwards
Sounds of Time Past

Form Follows Function | 56
1900–1980
Evolution of the Wristwatch

Made for the U.S.A. | 64
1854 onwards
American Patrons

Every Second Counts | 68
1862 onwards
Inventing the Chronograph

The Heart of the Machine | 72
1948–1985
The Quartz Watch

Future Meets Past | 76
1960 onwards
Enamel Painting Reborn

Modernity and Tradition | 82
1860–1975
The Lure of Complications

Time to Listen | 86
1860–1975
Grande and Petite Sonneries

Pushing the Limits of the Possible | 90
1860–1975
The Grand Complication

Family Ties | 94
1985 onwards
Fine-Tuning the Brand

Milestones | 98
1989–2020
Tradition and Innovation

Preface by Philippe Stern

1839　　　　　　1900　　　　　　　　　　　　　　2000

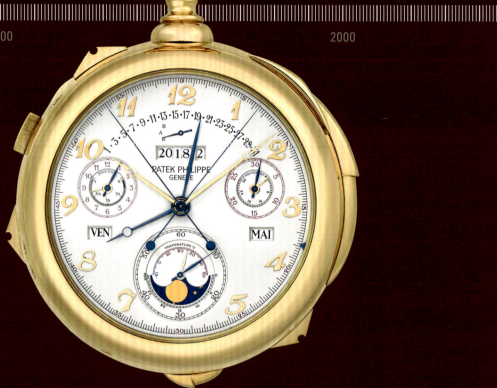

Precision and Beauty

This volume together with its companion volume provides new images and information on priceless treasures from the collections of the Patek Philippe Museum. Included are the company's own watches dating back to 1839, "The Patek Philippe Collection," which formed the core of the collection I started in the 1960s, and "The Antique Collection" with historic items that go back to the dawn of the portable timekeeper around 1500. Combined they represent a unique homage to Europe's horological heritage, for which I have long felt a passionate affinity. These books are intended for anyone, from generalists to experts, who is drawn to historic machines of unparalleled precision and beauty.

Each book might be compared to a play in twenty acts in chronological and thematic sequence. Each act is introduced by a concise historical account setting the scene. The stars of our drama are timepieces that have made history. All have been carefully auditioned (indeed chiming sonneries sing to you) by our expert curatorial team for their precision performance, dramatic presence, and beauty—a special beauty that not only resides on an enamel painted surface, but grows directly from choreographed motions of wheels and springs hidden within. These watches are masterpieces of form and function. Therefore, unlike most books of this type, we emphasize their inner mechanisms.

Representative artifacts document a confluence of aesthetics and technical genius in the mechanical watch. This complex history involves a constant dialog between innovation and tradition, which I regard as an essential tension. Nothing speaks more eloquently to this tension than the Calibre 89, introduced by Patek Philippe in 1989 in commemoration of the company's 150th anniversary. With its unprecedented 33 complications and revolutionary technologies, it is the superstar of the latter acts of our drama. But it also converses with the past, defying time itself and evoking time-honored traditions of the master watchmakers of the Vallée de Joux. Calibre 89 represented a major turning point in watchmaking that secured the success of the luxury mechanical watch in the face of ubiquitous, highly accurate, and inexpensive quartz watches, which ironically Patek Philippe had a hand in inventing.

Our books are dedicated to the creative spirits who have worked at our company over the past 183 years to realize the visions of our founders, Messieurs Patek and Philippe, to build the most precise and beautiful watches in the world.

Philippe Stern
Honorary Président, Patek Philippe SA

"The stars of our drama are timepieces that have made history."

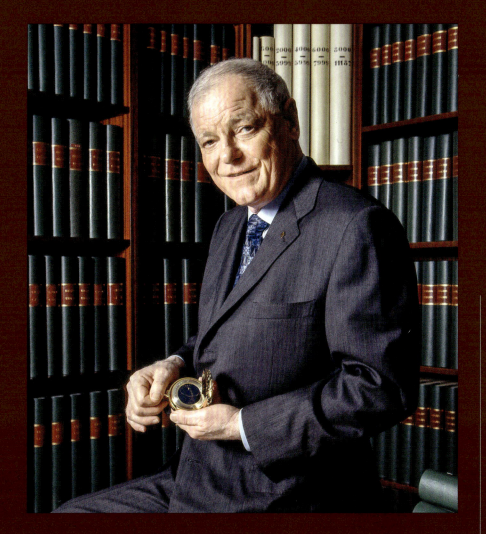

Philippe Stern in the Patek Philippe Archives, holding the Star Caliber 2000. Behind him are volumes documenting every watch produced by the company from 1839 onwards.

The watch shown on the left is the Calibre 89, which was in its day the most complicated watch ever built.

Patek, Philippe S.A.
Geneva, 1989
Caliber 32''', Prototype
Ø 88 mm; P-1989

Patek Philippe

1839   1900   2000

Quest for the Perfect Watch

The "perfect watch": that is the ideal that has driven the history of Patek Philippe since the beginning. Of course "perfect" means different things to different people at different times. This book explores what it means for Patek Philippe.

When Patek Philippe was founded in 1839, the Industrial Revolution was sweeping Europe, heralding an epoch of technological progress in power generation, manufacturing, communications, and transportation. Precision timekeeping was central to the revolution.

An innovation-driven company, Patek Philippe assembled a gifted staff that turned an 1845 patent by Jean Adrien Philippe (1815–1894) into the blockbuster watchmaking technology of the 19th century: a movement with a crown to wind the spring and set the hands. It is still the standard for mechanical watches today.

Beginning in 1948, the firm was a trailblazer for the electric watch and highly accurate quartz movements. By the 1970s, the dream of an autonomous watch that never had to be wound or reset seemed within reach. But when inexpensive Japanese quartz watches began to flood and disrupt the Swiss watch market, Patek Philippe decided to refocus on the mechanical watch. Starting in about 1980, they returned with a passion to what they had always done best:

building elegant watches with a traditional balance. Where Patek Philippe especially excelled and raised the bar was in the category of the "Grand Complication," a horological high-wire act of dozens of special functions, high elegance, and remarkable precision.

For Patek Philippe, the "perfect watch" was a seamless blend of art and technology, in which the true beauty of a timepiece comes from within, from a perfectly accurate mechanism. The watch became a symbol for the early 20th-century Machine Age and for a modernist aesthetic defined by the machine.

Investing strategically in watch case design, Patek Philippe revived endangered skills such as painting on enamel, among others. Without the company's support, such crafts would no longer exist. Patek Philippe remained the champion of the mechanical watch, their chosen vehicle of technological progress. With the fusion of innovation and tradition, of art and technology, Patek Philippe has its finger on the pulse of our time. The perfect watch, according to the slogan, is a treasure "You never actually own ... You merely look after it for the next generation."

Peter Friess
Director and Curator, Patek Philippe Museum

The true beauty of a timepiece
comes from within.

Antoine Norbert de Patek (1812–1877)
Lithograph
Geneva, circa 1860; V-7

Jean Adrien Philippe (1815–1894)
Lithograph
Geneva, circa 1860; V-8

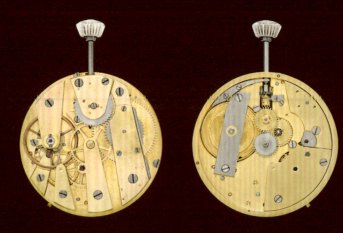

Origins of the Company

In 1839, two immigrants, Antoni Patek Prawdzic (1812–1877) from Poland and François Czapek (1811–after 1869) from Czechia, founded a watch company in Geneva. After the partnership dissolved in 1845, Patek, who had changed his name to Antoine Norbert de Patek, remained in Geneva, becoming a citizen of the city and integrating himself into the local culture.

In 1844, Patek had met the French watchmaker Jean Adrien Philippe (1815–1894) at the Exhibition of the Products of French Industry in Paris. National and international expositions played a major role in the Patek Philippe story.

At the exhibition Philippe introduced his new invention, a keyless winding and setting mechanism for watches (page 11, P-1842). Patek was quick to realize the potential of the invention, which forever changed the world of watches. In 1845, the French watchmaker joined him in partnership in Geneva. Patek, the astute entrepreneur, and Philippe, the watchmaker par excellence, shared a common vision of making the world's best, most complicated, most elegant watches.

In 1851, Philippe's name was added to the company, now known as "Patek, Philippe & Cie." It was an amazing success story: Two ambitious young immigrants ventured from their homelands to seek business opportunities in the newly formed Swiss Confederation. They were drawn to an informal network of highly skilled individual watchmakers, known as the "Fabrique genevoise."

Bringing together the talents of watchmakers in Geneva and the surrounding Jura Mountains, this production system went back at least 150 years. Distinguished by the division of labor and specialized craftsmanship associated with the Industrial Revolution, it was practiced by watchmakers from Geneva to La Chaux-de-Fonds.

Patek and Philippe capitalized on this local resource of skilled labor to create a worldwide market for their precision-made, beautifully designed watches. These innovative young entrepreneurs had begun to define a new and unique brand in watchmaking.

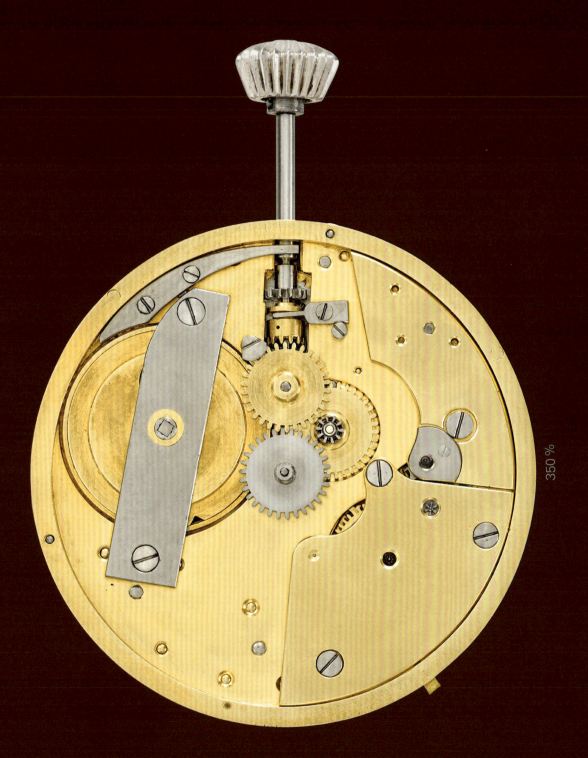

The Crown Supersedes the Key

This movement is the oldest surviving example of Jean Adrien Philippe's first combined crown-winding and setting mechanism: the crown can be turned to wind the mainspring and pulled to set the hands. A key is no longer needed.

Jean Adrien Philippe
Paris, 1842
Caliber 17'''
Ø 38 mm; P-1842

Era of the Industrial Revolution

1800   1839 1851   1900   2000

A Young Russian Nobleman

The back of this pendant watch with stem-winding and setting mechanism features the portrait of the young Paul Kisselew (1788–1872), a member of the Russian nobility, painted on enamel by Gaspard Lamunière (1810–1865) and framed by ramolayé and chiseled ornamentation, with flux finishing. Lamunière was one of the most important Genevan enamel painters in the 19th century. He worked frequently for Patek Philippe until the 1860s.

Patek & Cie – Fabricants à Genève
Geneva, 1845 (movement and case)
Caliber 14′′′, No. 1291
Ø 36 mm; P-12

Duke and King of Poland

The back of this pocket watch is engraved and highlighted with black enamel. It depicts the monument to Mieszko I (c. 930–992), Duke of Poland, and his son Boleslav I (967–1025), first king of Poland. The statue, by sculptor Christian Daniel Rauch (1777–1857), was erected in 1841 in the cathedral of Poznań in Poland.

Patek, Philippe & Cie –
Fabricants à Genève
Geneva, 1853 (movement), 1854 (case)
Caliber 18′′′, No. 8190
Ø 45 mm; P-1335

Polish Independence

Made for the Polish market, this pendant watch is engraved with the words "wynaleźli i zrobili" (patented invention), indicating that it uses Jean Adrien Philippe's stem-winding and setting mechanism. The front cover features the coat of arms of the alliance of Poland and Lithuania, which is a symbol of Poland's pursuit of independence, and a reference to Antoine Norbert de Patek's Polish origins. On the back cover, beneath a prince's crown and set in diamonds, are the initials "W B" of the owner of the watch.

Patek, Philippe & Cie –
Fabricants à Genève
Geneva, 1854 (movement), 1855 (case)
Caliber 13''', No. 9954
Ø 35 mm; P-42

Rhythms of Progress

1800　　　　　　　　1851　　　　　1894　　　　　　　　　　　　　　　　　2000

The Power of a Key(less) Invention

The 19th century was the great age of technological progress. An outpouring of inventions shaped our modern world of communication, transportation, and power, from the steamboat (1809) to the steam locomotive (1825), the telegraph (1833), the electric motor (1837), photography (1839) and other early image-making machines, the dynamo (1866), and the telephone (1876).

In 1842, the watch industry witnessed a game-changing invention: Jean Adrien Philippe's (1815–1894) system for winding and setting watches by means of the crown. Making the bothersome key obsolete once and for all, this revolutionary design captured the imagination of Antoine Norbert de Patek (1812–1877). But, as with all technology, this transition was gradual. For decades, key-wound devices persisted, running in parallel with Philippe's new paradigm. When Patek Philippe's first wristwatch appeared in 1868, it was a historic breakthrough, yet still used the old technology of a key to wind and set the hands (page 15, P-49).

In Patek Philippe's bid, beginning at mid-century, to capture and expand the luxury watch market, it produced every imaginable type of watch for its discerning international clientele: men's pocket watches, richly decorated in the techniques and styles of the day; watches with cabriolet cases; "form watches"; dainty women's pendant watches with enamel paintings or decorated with precious stones and pearls; singing-bird boxes; and even watches built into lorgnettes. Gradually, every one of these decorative pieces used Philippe's patented keyless stem-winding and setting mechanism, which soon became indispensable in every modern watch.

The crown—the cornerstone of Patek Philippe's innovative manufacturing system—signaled modernity. While the company relied as it always had on the unique skills of highly talented, independent Genevan craftsmen, it imposed on them a technological discipline to ensure quality. Watchmakers from Geneva and the nearby Jura Mountains applied their skillful hands and artistic imaginations to make cases, decorate them in the latest styles, and make movements that would fit exactly within their elegant cases. In the end, all of them had to work within the parameters of the keyless stem-winding and setting mechanism. Out of this emerged a near-perfect watch in which case and movement form a single, integrated unit.

The crown was the unique selling point that distinguished Patek Philippe's watches from those of their competitors. Between 1851 and 1890, watches with keys disappeared from Patek Philippe's production line. With the crown, the company secured its number one position in the watch industry.

Historic Breakthrough

250%

This is the first Patek Philippe wristwatch, a major milestone in the history of watchmaking. Made in 1868, it is notable for its stylish, historicist design and its tiny 15.5-millimeter movement, which started a trend in watchmaking. A ladies' watch, it was acquired by the Hungarian Countess Koscowicz. Wristwatches made for men would not be common for another forty years.

Patek, Philippe & Cie –
Fabricants à Genève
Geneva, 1868
Caliber 6''', No. 27 368
W. 32 mm; P-49

Rhythms of Progress

1800   1851   1894   2000

Duchess of Parma

This pendant watch with stem-winding and setting mechanism was sold on November 17, 1862, to the Duchess of Parma. Its back is set with nine amethysts and four rose-cut diamonds. The cuvette is enameled in translucent purple on an engine-turned ground to enhance the purple, or "parma," color of the amethysts.

Patek, Philippe & Cie – Fabricants à Genève
Geneva, 1859 (movement), 1860 (case)
Caliber 10''', No. 16 129
Ø 27 mm; P-1622

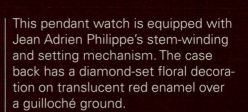

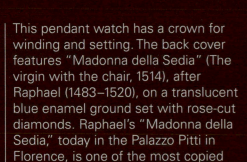

This pendant watch has a crown for winding and setting. The back cover features "Madonna della Sedia" (The virgin with the chair, 1514), after Raphael (1483–1520), on a translucent blue enamel ground set with rose-cut diamonds. Raphael's "Madonna della Sedia," today in the Palazzo Pitti in Florence, is one of the most copied works of the 18th and 19th centuries.

Patek & Cie – Fabricants à Genève
Geneva, 1850
Caliber 13''', No. 4592
Ø 35 mm; P-1131

This pendant watch is equipped with Jean Adrien Philippe's stem-winding and setting mechanism. The case back has a diamond-set floral decoration on translucent red enamel over a guilloché ground.

Patek & Cie – Fabricants à Genève
Geneva, 1848 (movement), 1850 (case)
Caliber 13''', Movement No. 3209
Ø 35 mm; P-1721

Raphael's Madonna

Translucence

Cabriolet

This simple pocket watch, equipped with the stem-winding and setting mechanism, can be turned in its cabriolet case for protection. With the dial facing outward, it is an open-faced watch; to shield the glass and make it a hunter-cased watch, the back can face outward.

Patek, Philippe & Cie –
Fabricants à Genève
Geneva, 1856 (movement), 1858 (case)
Caliber 16''', No. 12 858
Ø 50 mm; P-1451

Patek Philippe made approximately thirty lorgnette watches. This one has a traditional key-winding and setting mechanism. The case of this piece is engraved with scroll and floral motifs, and on the cover is a view of Geneva and Mont Blanc as seen from Pregny, enamel-painted by Bonnet. At a time of growing Swiss tourism, the enameled lid celebrates the Alpine beauty of the Geneva area.

Patek & Cie – Fabricants à Genève
Geneva, 1848 (movement), 1849 (case)
Caliber 9'''/15''', No. 3141
L. 97 mm; P-1559

View of Mont Blanc

Rhythms of Progress

1800 1851 1894 2000

Extra-fort Technique

The hunting scene on the back of this pocket watch was made with the "extra-fort" technique, which allowed for very thin, torsion-resistant cases with relatively little material. The silver is oxidized to turn black for contrast. The crown is extra-large for easier winding and setting.

Patek, Philippe & Cie –
Fabricants à Genève
Geneva, 1868 (movement), 1869 (case)
Caliber 11''', No. 35 085
Ø 49 mm; P-51

200 %

The 19th-century historicist style is displayed in this form watch evoking a medieval book, illuminated on its front cover with the Allegory of Drawing. The pendant watch has a key for winding and setting.

Patek, Philippe & Cie –
Fabricants à Genève
Geneva, 1869
Caliber 11''', No. 27 461
W. 24 mm; P-1190

Allegory of Drawing

Day and Night

The case of this pendant watch is decorated with the Allegory of the Day on one side, and the Allegory of the Night on the other. The two-marble relief tondi "Day" and "Night," crafted by Bertel Thorvaldsen (1770–1844) in 1815, are considered icons of neoclassical art. On this watch, they are presented in delicate enamel colors. The stem-winding and setting mechanism was an affirmation of modernity.

Patek, Philippe & Cie –
Fabricants à Genève
Geneva, 1872
Caliber 14''', No. 41 542
Ø 38 mm; P-494

This is one of the first miniature watches Patek Philippe equipped with a stem-winding and setting mechanism. Only six watches of this type were made. Small pendant watches were especially popular among female customers. Black versions were typically worn in mourning.

Patek, Philippe & Cie –
Fabricants à Genève
Geneva, 1857 (movement), 1862 (case)
Caliber 8''', No. 15 001
Ø 22 mm; P-566

150 %

Mourning

200 %

On the World Stage

Going to the Fairs

Patek Philippe's marketing strategy was crucial to its early corporate success. It was no accident that "Patek, Philippe & Cie," as it rebranded itself in 1851, began to gain global name recognition at the same time that the first World's Fair, the "Great Exhibition of the Works of Industry of All Nations," opened in London, running from May to October 1851. The world's nations and their manufacturers came together to display new products, submitting their best examples for prize competitions. Inventions of all types were on display, including daguerreotypes, an early fax machine, manufacturing and agricultural machinery, firearms, and vulcanized rubber. The Great Exhibition and world's fairs that followed were immensely important in promoting international trade. The fairs provided a grand stage for the Industrial Revolution.

The two entrepreneurs Patek (1812–1877) and Philippe (1815–1894) immediately understood the importance of world's fairs to their position in international business and always prepared meticulously for them. The London exhibition presented an unparalleled opportunity to showcase their products and to build their brand. As it turned out, the company made a grand showing, winning a gold medal for the quality and beauty of their watches.

Just as Samuel Colt's (1814–1862) exhibit of his prototype revolvers made with interchangeable parts put America on the map as an industrial force to be reckoned with, Patek Philippe kept Geneva on the map as an international watchmaking powerhouse.

Their exhibits awakened the interest of American retailers, then a new market for Swiss watches. Traveling to the U.S.A. in 1854, Patek came home with enough orders to keep the company busy for at least a year; an order from the important Tiffany & Co. in New York launched a business relationship that lasts to this day.

Queen Victoria (1819–1901), who formally opened London's Great Exhibition, bought from Patek Philippe a small, light blue pendant watch for herself and a hunter pocket watch with repeater for her husband, Prince Albert (1819–1861). Aristocrats and royal personages followed the queen's lead. Excited by their reception in London, the Genevan watchmaker adopted world's fairs as a central marketing platform for years to come (page 22, P-27).

Queen Victoria

Queen Victoria (1819–1901) paid several visits to the Great Exhibition in London in 1851—the first World's Fair. She greatly admired Patek Philippe's watches, especially for their innovative stem-winding and setting feature. Jean Adrien Philippe personally showed this pendant watch to her.

Patek, Philippe & Cie –
Fabricants à Genève
Geneva, 1850
Caliber 13''', No. 4536
Ø 33 mm; P-24

Queen Victoria by W. Warman after a painting by Thomas Sully from 1838; National Portrait Gallery, London

400 %

On the World Stage

1800　　　　　　1851　　　　　1900

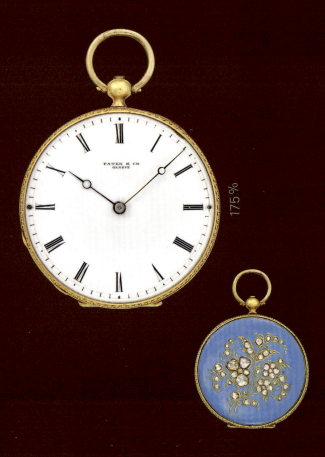

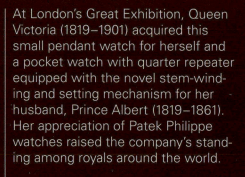

Queen of Denmark

At London's Great Exhibition, Queen Victoria (1819–1901) acquired this small pendant watch for herself and a pocket watch with quarter repeater equipped with the novel stem-winding and setting mechanism for her husband, Prince Albert (1819–1861). Her appreciation of Patek Philippe watches raised the company's standing among royals around the world.

Patek, Philippe & Cie –
Fabricants à Genève
Geneva, 1850 (movement), 1851 (case)
Caliber 12''', No. 4719
Ø 31 mm; P-27

This watch with stem-winding and setting mechanism was delivered in 1867 to Louise of Hesse-Kassel, Queen of Denmark (1817–1898), as a present for her husband Christian IX, King of Denmark (1818–1906), on their twenty-fifth wedding anniversary. Her portrait appears under the cover.

Patek, Philippe & Cie –
Fabricants à Genève
Geneva, 1866
Caliber 19''', No. 28 939
Ø 48 mm; P-1273

Victoria's Watch

22

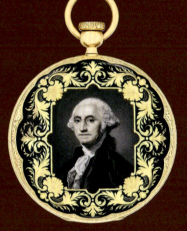
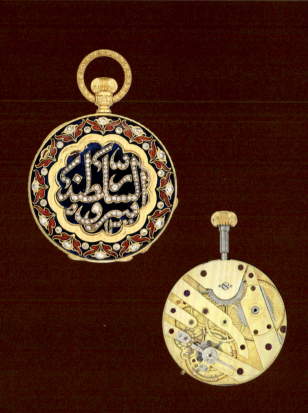

For a Persian Shah

The back of this pocket watch is decorated with a grisaille image of America's first president, George Washington (1732–1799), based on a famous portrait by Gilbert Stuart (1755–1828). The watch, equipped with a stem-winding and setting mechanism, was displayed at the Great Exhibition in London in 1851.

Patek, Philippe & Cie –
Fabricants à Genève
Geneva, 1850
Caliber 18''', No. 4035
Ø 45 mm; P-1412

This pendant watch was presented by the Persian Shah Mozzafar-al-Din Shah Qajar (1853–1907) to his wife Surur al-Saltanah. The front cover is engine-turned, enameled in blue, and set with rose-cut diamonds that form her name in Arabic calligraphy. The decorated back bears the date: 1300 of the Hegira (1882–1883), in Arabic calligraphy. The watch has a crown for winding and setting.

Patek, Philippe & Cie,
Société en nom collectif
Geneva, 1883
Caliber 15''', No. 49 133
Ø 39 mm; P-1693

Patek Philippe delivered this lavishly jeweled pendant watch to Tiffany & Co. in New York in 1852. Diamonds against a deep blue background evoke a star-studded American flag. By 1849, the American retailer had ordered six watches from Patek Philippe. This piece uses the traditional winding and setting mechanism with a key.

Patek, Philippe & Cie –
Fabricants à Genève
Geneva, 1850 (movement), 1852 (case)
Caliber 14''', No. 4740
Ø 38 mm; P-1658

George Washington

Star-Spangled

23

1873   1968   2000

Chronometers and Observatory Trials

Punctuality is a major concern of modern industrial society. Accurate watches, considered the epitome of precision, were key to the Industrial Revolution. Patek Philippe built the most accurate timekeepers in the world and early on set the pace in the highly competitive watch market. Before quartz technology in the 1970s drastically lowered the prices for accurate watches, customers had to pay a premium for this precision.

The initial drivers for timekeeping accuracy were the practical needs of navigation, scientific measurement, modern time-and-motion studies, and, not least, competitive sports. Fractions of a second, tenths, hundredths, and thousandths of a second were the new units of modernity.

Chronometers are extremely precise timekeepers. Their manufacture pushed watchmakers ever closer to the limits of their capabilities. Formal external validations of precision became standard procedure, with major astronomical observatories taking the lead. In 1873, the Geneva Observatory set up and served as judges for a watch competition with strict rules. Participating companies of course had to submit their timepieces anonymously for rigorous evaluation over several weeks.

By the 20th century, observatory-tested watches played a critical role in timing Olympic events. Conversely, the chronometer trials, which continued until 1968, themselves became a kind of Olympiad for precision watches where superstar "adjusters" were responsible for the critical fine-tuning. In Geneva Observatory competitions between 1900 and 1950, Patek Philippe received 1,728 prizes—more than all other watch companies combined. Over the years, the firm garnered 325 First Prizes, which reinforced their undisputed market position. They had a spectacular year in 1884, for example, when they dominated competition by winning the first five places.

Accuracy was of utmost importance, especially the ability to stay accurate over long periods of time. Patek Philippe aimed for nothing less than absolute precision—the "perfect watch"— such that a watch never had to be reset. It would show the correct time forever and ever.

Precision Record

Crafted in 1930, this pocket chronometer with lever escapement and one-minute tourbillon set a precision record in the 1962 Geneva Observatory competition—a record that still stands. French for "whirlwind," the tourbillon is a rotating cage containing the balance and parts of the escapement, ensuring the constant frequency of the balance. It was awarded a "Record de pièce" and "Bulletin de Première Classe" with "First Prize" mention.

Patek, Philippe & Cie,
Société Anonyme
Geneva, 1930 (movement),
1951 (case), 1983 (dial and hands)
Reference 810, Caliber 17''',
Movement No. 198 411
Ø 48 mm; P-424

In Pursuit of Precision

| 1800 | 1873 | 1968 | 2000 |

Jump-Hour Chronometer

Deck chronometers like this were designed for ship navigation. It is likely Patek Philippe's only jump-hour chronometer with power reserve and lever escapement, and it won multiple prizes at Geneva Observatory competitions. The hours are indicated in a small aperture over the center of the dial.

Patek, Philippe & Cie,
Société Anonyme
Geneva, 1919 (movement), 1926 (case)
Caliber 22''', Movement No. 191 439
Ø 60 mm; P-163

250 %

Tourbillon in a Wrist Chronometer

This wrist chronometer with lever escapement may be the first ever to contain a tourbillon. Its movement is one of the most precise ever made. Originally patented in 1801 by Abraham-Louis Breguet (1747–1823), the tourbillon ranks as one of the greatest feats in watchmaking. As the balance swings, the tourbillon cage spins on its axis once a minute, compensating for any imbalances within the escapement.

Patek, Philippe & Cie, S.A.
Geneva, 1949 (movement), 1987 (case)
Reference 3699, 30 mm Observatory
Caliber, Movement No. 861 115
Ø 39 mm; P-709

Top Award

The wrist chronometer with straight-line lever escapement is driven by a 30-millimeter observatory caliber, designed for the Geneva Observatory competition. In 1955, it won a top award in the small caliber category.

Patek, Philippe & Cie, S.A.
Geneva, 1954 (movement), 1955 (case)
Reference 2556, 30 mm Observatory
Caliber, Movement No. 861 137
Ø 38 mm; P-789

In Pursuit of Precision

| 1800 | 1873 | 1968 | 2000 |

Bulletin de Première Classe

This skeleton deck chronometer is equipped with a lever escapement and one-minute tourbillon regulator. Adjusted by master adjuster François Modoux in 1929 and 1930, it received a "Bulletin de Première Classe" with "Second Prize" mention at the 1929 timing contest of the Geneva Observatory in Category A. The movement was skeletonized and engraved in 1980.

Patek, Philippe & Cie,
Société Anonyme
Geneva, 1922 (movement), 1981 (case)
Reference 922, Caliber 22''',
Movement No. 197 670
Ø 65 mm; P-425

28

Major Challenge

This wrist chronometer has a lever escapement and a 50-second tourbillon regulator. Caliber 34 T was developed in the 1950s for Geneva Observatory competition in Category D for small watches. It was a major challenge to fit a tourbillon into such a small movement.

Patek, Philippe & Cie, S.A.
Geneva, 1956 (movement), 1983 (case)
Reference 3834, Caliber 34 T,
Movement No. 866 503
W. 29 mm; P-426

Innovations in Marketing

1872   1936   2000

Exporting to South America

Having successfully established relationships in North America, Patek Philippe turned to South America beginning in 1872, when it started to work with the Brazilian retailer Gondolo & Labouriau. It found a ready partner in a country which was becoming open to the design ideas of modern architects like Oscar Niemeyer (1907–2012). By the 1920s, Brazilian artists were enthusiastically importing European Modernism, giving it a very distinct Brazilian accent.

In March 1902, Patek Philippe registered the trade name "Chronometro Gondolo" for a type of pocket watch with special technical features produced exclusively for the Brazilian retailer. In the 1920s, Gondolo & Labouriau also began to order wristwatches from the Genevan company. The collaboration reached its peak between 1902 and 1913. Their varied designs reflected the spirit of creativity and experimentation in the early years of the wristwatch. The designs of the Chronometro Gondolo watches expressed the emerging modernist style.

Creativity was also on display in the Brazilian retailer's novel marketing methods. A legendary Patek Philippe loyalty club organized festive picnics with original music like the "Patek Waltz"—its signature tune—played at the event, anticipating modern direct marketing techniques. Club members did not have to be rich, royal, or famous to join. It was enough to be an enthusiast for a movement that stood for innovation and elegant modern design. Club members could buy their own Patek Philippe timepiece on an installment plan and even win one through a clever lottery scheme. This was perhaps the most uncommon marketing ploy in the world of luxury watches, showing Patek Philippe's openness to unconventional approaches.

The collaboration between Gondolo & Labouriau and Patek Philippe lasted for sixty-four years, from 1872 to 1936. Amazingly, for the quarter century between 1902 and the Great Depression, the Brazilian retailer absorbed nearly a third of the entire production, making Patek Philippe a familiar name not only in Brazil but across South America.

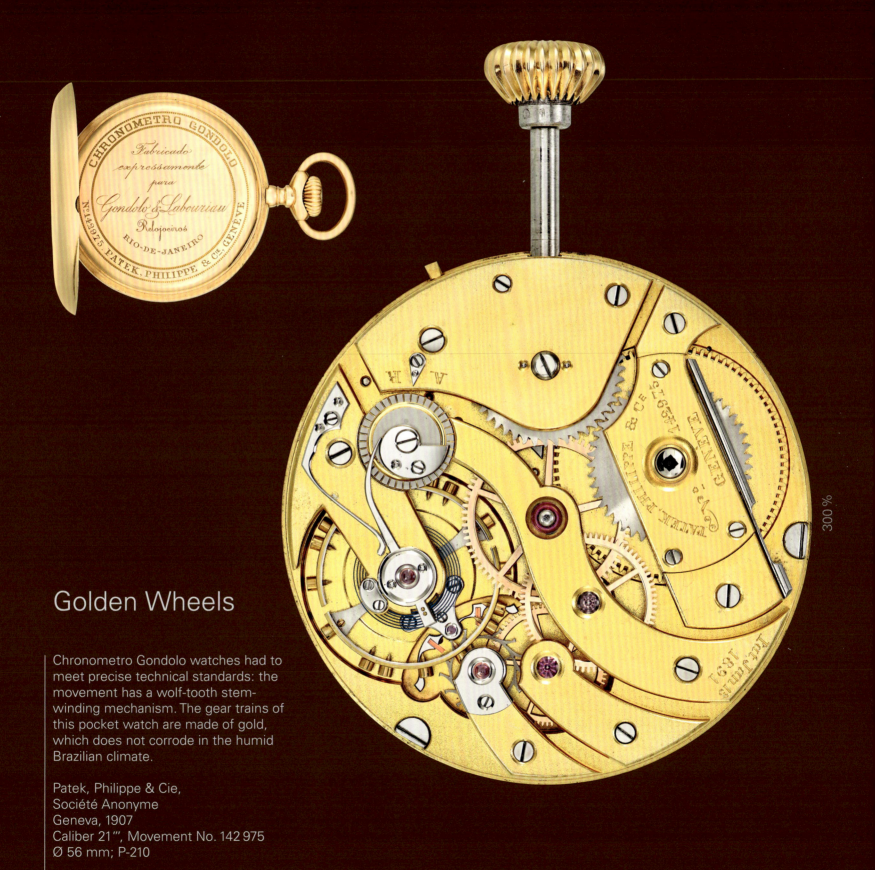

Golden Wheels

Chronometro Gondolo watches had to meet precise technical standards: the movement has a wolf-tooth stem-winding mechanism. The gear trains of this pocket watch are made of gold, which does not corrode in the humid Brazilian climate.

Patek, Philippe & Cie,
Société Anonyme
Geneva, 1907
Caliber 21''', Movement No. 142 975
Ø 56 mm; P-210

Innovations in Marketing

1800   1872   1936   2000

Trademarking

The name "Chronometro Gondolo," as on this 24-hour pocket watch, was trademarked in Switzerland in 1902. The practice of trademarking was unprecedented in the history of Patek Philippe, and was a special mark of distinction for its Brazilian retailer.

Patek, Philippe & Cie,
Société Anonyme
Geneva, 1907
Caliber 20''' Gondolo type,
Movement No. 146 699
Ø 51 mm; P-436

Golden Gondolo

This oversized wristwatch with a gold tonneau-shaped case was delivered to Gondolo & Labouriau on February 15, 1921. The movement meets the exclusive technical specifications for a Gondolo-type watch.

Patek, Philippe & Cie,
Société Anonyme
Geneva, 1913 (movement), 1920 (case)
Caliber 12''' Gondolo type,
Movement No. 180 780
W. 30 mm; P-1322

200 %

Art Deco

The movement of this Chronometro Gondolo dress watch was originally housed in a different case. On January 4, 1928, at the request of Relojoaria Gondolo, the movement was fitted into the present case during servicing by Patek Philippe; the case, the dial, and the engravings with black enamel accents were then adapted to the Art Deco style.

Patek, Philippe & Cie,
Société Anonyme
Geneva, 1911 (movement), 1928 (case)
Caliber 12''' Gondolo type,
Movement No. 167 624
W. 30 mm; P-840

Conversions

This rectangular wristwatch, large for the 1920s, was delivered on November 9, 1922, to Gondolo & Labouriau. Its movement of the Gondolo type had originally been made for a pendant watch.

Patek, Philippe & Cie,
Société Anonyme
Geneva, 1913 (movement), 1920 (case)
Caliber 12''' Gondolo type,
Movement No. 180 708
W. 30 mm; P-1134

Perpetual Calendars

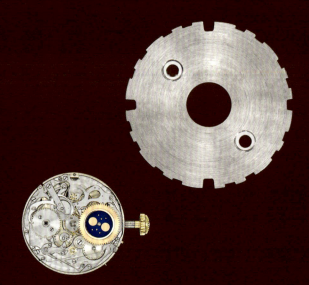

Patek Philippe reveled in the exploratory spirit of the Machine Age. It struck out into new and unknown territory in the development of highly accurate mechanical calendars, one of the most challenging of all horological "complications." The goal was to produce a complex gear train that drastically reduced the need to adjust the calendar.

Early in its history, the firm was equipping pocket watches with mechanical calendars. The weekday, date and month, and sometimes the year and phases of the moon were assigned their own hands, windows, and symbols on the dial. Simple movements required resetting the calendar on the first day of each month.

The company then produced an automated annual calendar, although it still had to be corrected on the first of March, since the watch was not yet capable of accounting for Februarys with 28 or 29 days. Patek Philippe took a major step forward with the so-called "perpetual calendar," which only needed to be adjusted on centennial years that are not leap years—that is, only three times in every 400 years. In 1925, a milestone in watch history, Patek Philippe was the first firm to succeed in equipping the smaller wristwatch with a perpetual calendar (page 35, P-72).

Patek Philippe then pushed the technology further with the "secular" calendar, which also included leap centennial years in the calculations. In principle, watch owners would not have to touch a secular calendar in their lifetimes, nor would their heirs (page 37, P-421).

This modern watch complication was based on very old knowledge, going back to the Julian calendar created in Rome over 2,000 years ago and the Gregorian calendar in the Renaissance almost 500 years ago. Patek Philippe was able to capture this knowledge in the algorithms programmed into its mechanical calendars: It produced a Machine Age wonder that was a major step toward its ultimate vision of a perfect, fully autonomous watch—one that in principle worked without human intervention for time eternal.

Milestone

Made from 1898 to 1925, this is the first wristwatch with a perpetual calendar—a milestone in watchmaking. It always shows the correct date, even in leap years. For over 250 years, the invention of a movement with a reliable perpetual calendar posed a major, but not insurmountable, problem to watchmakers. Fitting it into a small wristwatch was extremely difficult.

Pictured on the facing page is the cam storing the program for the perpetual calendar over four years. The depth of the notches relates to months with 28, 29, 30, and 31 days.

Patek, Philippe & Cie,
Société en nom collectif
Geneva, 1898 (movement), 1925 (case)
Caliber 12''', Movement No. 97 975
Ø 34 mm; P-72

Tracking Time Eternal

1800　　　　　　　　1861　　　　1900　　　　　　　　　　　　　　　　　　　2000

Reference 1505

The three small apertures on the dial of this wristwatch show the day of the week, the month, and the date in French. The clear design is in the Art Deco style.

Patek, Philippe & Cie, S.A.
Geneva, 1938 (movement), 1941 (case)
Reference 1505, Caliber 12-120,
Movement No. 828 665
Ø 33 mm; P-1171

Reference 1518

This perpetual calendar chronograph, reference 1518, was the world's first serially produced perpetual calendar chronograph. It became an instant success, redefining the general look of Patek Philippe wristwatches with complications for decades.

Patek, Philippe & Cie, S.A.
Geneva, 1942
Reference 1518, Caliber 13-130,
Movement No. 862 854
Ø 44 mm; P-696

Reference 1526

In 1941, Patek Philippe became the first company to initiate serial production of wristwatches with a perpetual calendar. This watch, reference 1526, is the prototype.

Patek, Philippe & Cie, S.A.
Geneva, 1941
Reference 1526, Caliber 12''',
Movement No. 921 373
Ø 35 mm; P-1272

Secular Calendar

This pocket watch has dials on both front and back. The secular calendar on the back takes into account secular years that are not leap years: 2100, 2200, 2300, 2500, 2600, 2700, etc.; the years 2000, 2400, and 2800 must be manually corrected. Only three watches of this type were built.

This cam carries the program for the secular calendar over 400 years. The depth of the notches relates to months with 28, 29, 30, and 31 days. The levers ensure that certain centennials are not shown as leap years.

Patek, Philippe S.A.
Geneva, 1973 (movement), 1973 (case)
Reference 871, Caliber 17-170,
Movement No. 932 194
Ø 54 mm; P-421

Embracing Modernism

1800　　　　　　　　　　　　　1890　　　　　1932　　　　　　　　　　　　　　　2000

Art Nouveau and Art Deco

In the early 1900s, Patek Philippe produced watches richly decorated in the Art Nouveau and Art Deco styles, the prevailing art and design movements of the era. Variants of Modernism, they framed the cultural upheavals of the First World War—a chaos that destroyed so many pre-war structures and traditions.

Emerging around 1890, Art Nouveau was identified with colorful and curvaceous forms that imitated the shape of living plants and flowers in the medium of modern, industrial materials. In many ways, it was sui generis. And yet, its streamlined look reflected the industrial aesthetic, according to the modernist form-follows-function dictum. Art Deco, coming on its heels and peaking in the interwar years, leaned more toward sharp, geometric lines. It was a style found in commonly used products.

Patek Philippe straddled both design movements. As Art Nouveau evolved into Art Deco, their timepieces from the 1930s reflect the mechanization of everyday life, yet they still evoke the sensuousness of Art Nouveau. Watches of that time became archetypes of the modern machine aesthetic.

The 41 years between 1891 and 1932 saw Patek Philippe's transition from its founding generation of owners. Jean Adrien Philippe (1815–1894) retired in 1891, dying soon after, although his descendants remained active in the business until 1933. Antoine Norbert de Patek (born 1812) had died in 1877. His children were not active in the company.

In 1932, Patek Philippe was acquired by its present owners, the Stern family, who had long been major suppliers of its dials. They were thus deeply familiar with the company's goals and values. They maintained the Patek Philippe tradition of producing the most precise, complicated, elegant timepieces in the world. They continued to embrace the machine aesthetic, particularly Art Deco, stamping their brand with Modernism, their signature style even today.

Marquis de Lafayette

The Marquis de Lafayette (1757–1834), whose image appears on this pocket watch, came from an ancient French aristocratic family. Pursuing his strong beliefs in democracy and human rights, Lafayette fought in the American Revolutionary War (1775–1783) and in the French Revolution (1789) for his principles. He is sometimes called "the hero of two worlds."

Patek, Philippe & Cie,
Société Anonyme
Geneva, 1916 (movement), 1917 (case)
Caliber 17''', Movement No. 187 744
W. 44 mm; P-1732

Embracing Modernism

| 1800 | 1890 | 1932 | 2000 |

Flower Power

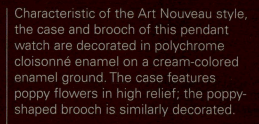

Characteristic of the Art Nouveau style, the case and brooch of this pendant watch are decorated in polychrome cloisonné enamel on a cream-colored enamel ground. The case features poppy flowers in high relief; the poppy-shaped brooch is similarly decorated.

Patek, Philippe & Cie,
Société en nom collectif
Geneva, 1900 (movement), 1901 (case)
Caliber 10′′′, Movement No. 115 212
Ø 27 mm; P-1566

Floral Splendor

The delicately crafted floral patterns on this dress watch are reminiscent of Art Nouveau.

Patek, Philippe & Cie,
Société Anonyme
Geneva, 1970 (movement), 1925 (case)
Caliber 17-140, Movement No. 893 357
Ø 44 mm; P-99

200 %

Egypt Craze

This pocket watch was sold in 1922, during the Egypt craze following the discovery of King Tutankhamun's tomb. The enamel painting portrays the Egyptian god "Geb."

Patek, Philippe & Cie,
Société en nom collectif
Geneva, 1910 (movement), 1911 (case)
Caliber 17''' ultra-thin,
Movement No. 162 517
Ø 45 mm; P-1738

Minimalism

The dial is a wonder of Art Deco simplicity, with the hour hand replaced by a tiny aperture. This is the only platinum jump-hour pocket watch known to have been made by Patek Philippe.

Patek, Philippe & Cie,
Société Anonyme
Geneva, 1921
Caliber 17''', Movement No. 199 933
Ø 45 mm; P-1415

41

Embracing Modernism

1800 | 1890 | 1932 | 2000

Dancing Diamonds

The ornamentation, case, and crown of this pendant watch are made of platinum, which was still new as a material for jewelry. Yet the rare white metal brought out the glitter of the diamonds on this watch and was well suited to Art Deco.

Patek, Philippe & Cie,
Société Anonyme
Geneva, 1910
Caliber 9''', Movement No. 158 926
W. 40 mm; P-1064

Pop-up Watch

When the covers "à volets" of the gold Art Deco case of this purse or night-table watch are opened, the watch pops up. The hand for the seconds turns on a subsidiary dial at 6 o'clock.

Patek, Philippe & Cie,
Société Anonyme
Geneva, 1919 (movement), 1932 (case)
Caliber 9''', Movement No. 192 438
W. 39 mm; P-1602

Octagonal Attraction

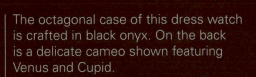

The octagonal case of this dress watch is crafted in black onyx. On the back is a delicate cameo shown featuring Venus and Cupid.

Patek, Philippe & Cie,
Société Anonyme
Geneva, 1921 (movement), 1922 (case)
Caliber 12''' ultra-flat,
Movement No. 805 957
W. 46 mm; P-103

Jumping Forward in Time

1800　　　　1840　　　　　　　　1913　　　　　　　　　　　　　　2000

One of Jean Adrien Philippe's Last Patents

An "independent jumping seconds" pocket watch was one of Jean Adrien Philippe's (1815–1894) final patents. Swiss patent number 1017 was awarded to him in 1889, only five years before his death. The first thing to notice in the watch is a second hand that jumps from one second to the next with an audible click. Today we are used to such displays in analog quartz watches but seldom in their mechanical equivalents, because of the technical challenges involved. Philippe's invention also allows for stopping and starting the second hand in order to measure very brief events. One can either observe the second hand make its jumps or count the clicks.

A similar mechanism had been invented a century earlier by the Genevan watchmaker Jean-Moïse Pouzait (1753–1793). He, too, could stop the second hand, but unfortunately the other hands were stopped as well. For his jumping second hand, he used a large balance wheel which vibrated once per second and advanced the second hand exactly one second.

Jean Adrien Philippe improved on Pouzait's ideas. He made the second hand independent of the rest of the watch, giving it its own gear train. The movement for the hours and minutes used a regular small balance, which makes two and a half swings per second, after which the jumping hand is released to move forward by one second. The advantages are, one, that the small balance is not easily thrown out of its rhythm; and, two, the second hand could be stopped without stopping the hour and minute hands. He also added another hand on the dial, which, in sync with the natural rate of the balance, records fifths of a second—rotating too fast for the eye to follow.

Jean Adrien Philippe had been working on this mechanism since the 1840s, from the beginning of his career with the manufacturer. Along with the crown for winding and setting the watch, it was another invention in pursuit of the "perfect watch."

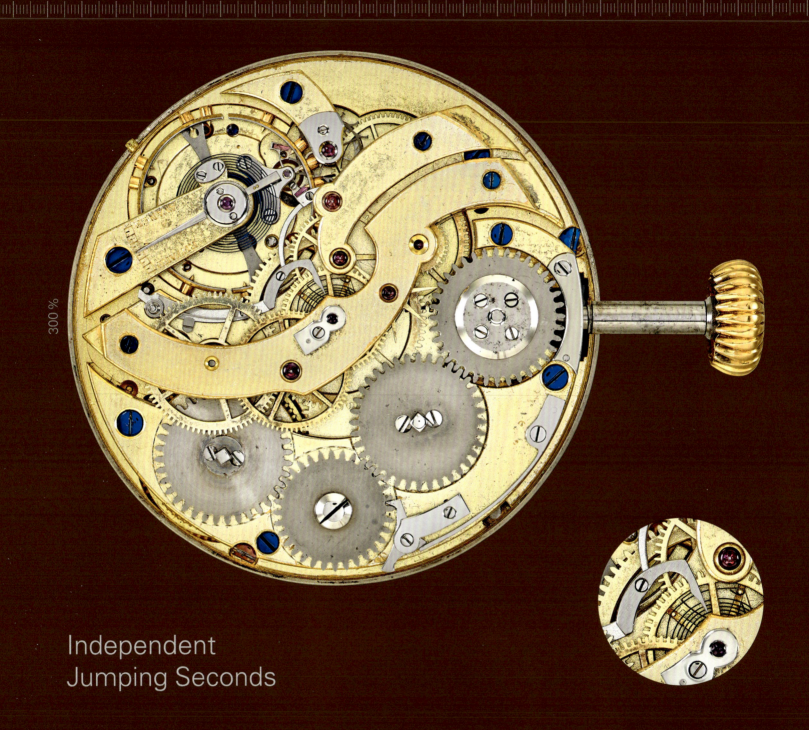

Independent Jumping Seconds

This pocket watch with independent jumping seconds and flyback is the most complicated of Patek Philippe's watches of this type.

Patek, Philippe & Cie –
Fabricants à Genève
Geneva, 1867
Caliber 20''', Movement No. 27 171
Ø 55 mm; P-1224

Chasing Time Around a Faster World

1900　　　　　1937　　　　　2000

World Time Watches

For many centuries, local time was determined by the position of the sun, with noon defined as the time when the sun reaches its highest point in the sky. Thus each longitude had its own noon, resulting in a multitude of local times that varied from each other as one moved in an easterly or westerly direction. But this was not a problem for most people in times past. The vast majority lived in one place and stayed there, perfectly comfortable in their local times. When people traveled, it was at a leisurely pace.

All of this changed around 1825 with the rise of the railroad. Locations once separated by a multi-day coach ride could now be reached in a matter of hours. The patchwork of local times made it impossible to develop useful railway timetables. Establishing reliable rail connections for faster and faster trains required an overhaul of the time system. Instituted by international agreement in 1883, Standard Time divided the world into official time zones. Accordingly, travelers needed new timekeepers, and the industry responded. Additional dials and hands as well as rotating rings and discs made it much easier to navigate in the new world time system.

In the 20th century, time took on a whole new dimension with transportation breakthroughs like the airplane. Talking on the telephone bridged time zones with the speed of light. The world became suddenly smaller in the late 1930s with the beginning of international air travel. The communications revolution made it even smaller.

Subdials and other travel-friendly indicators on watches dramatically increased. In 1937 Patek Philippe launched the first wristwatch showing the current time at selected locations around the world. With this special complication, a world time watch effectively became several watches in one. And for Patek Philippe, this was another significant step on the road to the "perfect watch" (page 47, P-938).

Cottier's Creation

Louis Cottier (1894–1966) built his first mechanism for the "Heure Universelle" (world time) in 1937. He added some parts to an existing Patek Philippe movement from 1925. The pink 24-hour ring turns counter-clockwise every 24 hours and shows the 24 time zones for the cities listed on the white outer dial. The mechanism developed by Cottier earned him a place in history as the "father of the modern world time watch."

Patek, Philippe & Cie, S.A.
Geneva, 1925 (movement), 1937 (case)
Reference 515 HU, Caliber 10''',
Movement No. 811 161
W. 26 mm; P-938

150 %

Chasing Time Around a Faster World

1800　　　　　　　　　　　1900　　　**1937**　　　　　2000

Gold Medalist

Double Dial

Double Time

A pocket watch with independent seconds, second local time, and minute repeating, this piece was presented at the 1867 Universal Exhibition in Paris. At the time of production, it was one of the most complicated watches ever made by the company. Patek Philippe was awarded a gold medal at the fair.

Patek, Philippe & Cie –
Fabricants à Genève
Geneva, 1864
Caliber 21''', Movement No. 24 139
Ø 56 mm; P-902

This wristwatch adds a special blue hour hand for a second time zone, using two push buttons to set the time back or forward by one hour.

Patek, Philippe & Cie, S.A.
Geneva, 1962 (movement), 1959 (case)
Reference 2597 HS, Caliber 12-400 HS,
Movement No. 729 427
Ø 35 mm; P-97

This self-winding wristwatch shows the time in two time zones simultaneously. The dial on the right shows the current local time and the one on the left another time zone.

Patek, Philippe & Cie, S.A.
Geneva, 1963 (movement), 1961 (case)
Reference 3452, Caliber 27-460,
Movement No. 1 111 350
Ø 39 mm; P-1548

41 Cities

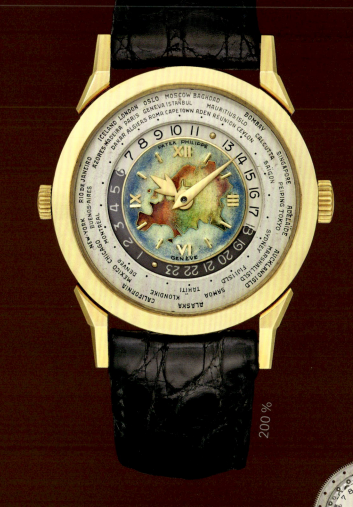

Globetrotter

The black-and-white 24-hour ring on the dial of this world time wristwatch rotates counterclockwise and indicates the time zones of 41 locations around the world. It also shows if it is day or night time at each location.

Patek, Philippe & Cie, S.A.
Geneva, 1944 (movement), 1945 (case)
Reference 1415 HU, Caliber 12-120 HU,
Movement No. 926 077
Ø 31 mm; P-461

On the dial on this world time wristwatch, made in 1953 for Patek Philippe by Louis Cottier (1894–1966), is a map of Eurasia. The second crown at 9 o'clock is used to set the outer ring to the desired city in order to find its local time.

Patek, Philippe & Cie, S.A.
Geneva, 1953
Reference 2523 HU, Caliber 12-400 HU,
Movement No. 720 303
Ø 36 mm; P-1148

Paradox of Modernity

1839　　　　　　　　　　1900　　　　　　　　　　　　　　　　　2000

Sounds of Time Past

When the first mechanical clocks appeared in the 13th century on towers, they had neither dials nor hands, but they did strike bells. These ordered the day for the medieval city. The ringing of the bells was a familiar sound.

A repeater—a complication found in high-end watches—makes time audible, as a rule, on demand. Low tones mark the hours, high and low tones the quarter hours, half-quarter hours, ten or five minutes, and even the minutes. Patek Philippe invested heavily in repeater watches. At London's Great Exhibition of 1851, the company made a splash with a pocket watch equipped with a repeater as well as Jean Adrien Philippe's invention of the crown for winding and setting the timepiece. In 1916, the company succeeded in crafting a five-minute repeater small enough to fit into a women's wristwatch (page 51, P-594).

Their repeater wristwatches are prized for their purity of sound. So important is the quality of sound to the current president that Thierry Stern (born 1970), as did his father before him, personally listens to and approves every minute repeater the company produces. Although miniaturization posed a huge technical challenge, the elegance of the movement and case remained a priority. The watch was crafted as an integrated artwork.

The sounds of repeaters had lost the presence they once had in the church, at work, or at home. Still, they remained in demand. Was it all just a gimmick? If it was, it was a seductive one. The gongs, harking back to the earliest days of watchmaking, sparked powerful memories. Yet, as the watches show, they were modern mechanical masterpieces. To craft a repeater required no less technical know-how than a chronometer did. This type of technical progress that is directed toward bygone times is a paradox of modernity. It was a form of techno-nostalgia, a tension between a thrust toward the future and a pull toward a familiar and comfortable past.

5-Minute Repeater

This ladies' watch is the first Patek Philippe wristwatch with a repeater, a complication that sounds the time on demand. This specimen is a 5-minute repeater. Its two gongs are activated by the slider on the case band. The movement was based on a raw ébauche built in the Vallée de Joux and finished in Patek Philippe's workshops on the Rue du Rhône in Geneva.

Patek, Philippe & Cie,
Société Anonyme
Geneva, 1916
Caliber 10''', Movement No. 174 603
Ø 27 mm; P-594

Paradox of Modernity

1800　　　1839　　　　　1900　　　　　　　　　　　　2000

Feeling Time

With this very early "à tact" pendant watch, feeling with your fingertips the position of the large gold watch-hand in relation to the hour-indicator knobs allowed you to tell the time without seeing the dial. The watch also has a quarter-hour repeater marking the time audibly. Patek Philippe began making à tact watches, with and without striking mechanisms, around 1845, and displayed them at the London Great Exhibition of 1851.

Patek & Cie – Fabricants à Genève
Geneva, 1845
Caliber 14''', Movement No. 1325
Ø 39 mm; P-670

The Deer Hunt

This quarter-repeater pocket watch was presented at the 1851 Universal Exhibition in London. On demand, it strikes the hours and the quarters on two gongs. The back of the yellow gold case is chased in high relief with the scene of a deer hunt.

Patek & Cie – Fabricants à Genève
Geneva, 1850
Caliber 18''', Movement No. 3925
Ø 46 mm; P-1037

The Lure of Lalique

This pocket watch is a minute repeater and has differential winding. René Lalique (1860–1945), master artist and jeweler of the Art Nouveau period, decorated the watch case with chased and enameled front and back, featuring rhinoceros beetles and trumpet flower designs. Very few watches decorated by Lalique exist. His fame in jewelry design dates from 1895.

Patek, Philippe & Cie,
Société en nom collectif
Geneva, 1895 (movement), 1900 (case)
Caliber 18''', Movement No. 97 537
Ø 49 mm; P-1159

Paradox of Modernity

1800　　　　　　　　1839　　　　　　　　　　　1900　　　　　　　　　　　　　　　　2000

Alhambra

This 5-minute repeating pendant watch sounds the time at 5-minute intervals. Yet beauty was not sacrificed to technical flash. The front cover is enameled with the name "Ygnacia" on a pink ground, and the back cover is enameled with a view of the Alhambra in Granada, Spain.

Patek, Philippe & Cie,
Société en nom collectif
Geneva, 1890 (movement), 1891 (case)
Caliber 14''', Movement No. 90 172
Ø 39 mm; P-1642

150 %

250 %

Minute-urization

This ladies' pendant watch has a minute repeater. Fitting it into such a small movement was extremely difficult. Originally housed in a rose gold case, the present yellow gold and platinum American-made case dates from the early 20th century. It is entirely pavé-set with rose-cut diamonds centered on a ruby motif.

Patek, Philippe & Cie,
Société en nom collectif
Geneva, 1892
Caliber 10''', Movement No. 97 012
Ø 30 mm; P-128

250 %

Fashion for Men

This early minute-repeating wristwatch for men features a then-very fashionable rectangular case with tortue lugs. The movement was equipped with a gong spring in 1926, and the watch was sold in 1927.

Patek, Philippe & Cie,
Société Anonyme
Geneva, 1917 (movement), 1926 (case)
Caliber 12''', Movement No. 174 709
W. 30 mm; P-739

1800   1900   1980   2000

Evolution of the Wristwatch

The wristwatch is the direct descendant of the pocket watch. At the turn of the 20th century, both types co-existed. But the wristwatch gained currency in the First World War, because soldiers found it more efficient to steal a quick glance at the wrist than to reach into the pocket. In 1923, Patek Philippe considered committing itself to the wristwatch. In short order, in fact, that became the backbone of its business. The trend toward wristwatches was unstoppable, and within a few decades they outnumbered pocket watches fifty to one. But just as early automobiles evolved from and, consequently, partially resembled horse-drawn carriages, early wristwatches showed vestiges of their pocket watch origins.

The transition from the pocket and neck to the wrist forced technical innovations. There was not only the challenge of reducing the size of the movement, but also of building sturdier cases to protect the delicate mechanism in its unpocketed position from exposure to water, dust, and magnetic fields. The new location also provided a technical advantage: the natural motion of the wrist assisted the self-winding feature.

No one company can be credited with the invention of the wristwatch; many saw the potential for a huge market. But Patek Philippe put its own stamp on the new devices, developing special functions like chronographs, calendars, and striking mechanisms. For watches without complications, which showed only hours, minutes, and seconds, style and fashion became paramount considerations.

The wristwatch gained further momentum in the 1930s, when Patek Philippe's designers developed a distinct in-house style based on Art Deco; it was in keeping with current fashion but still unmistakably their own. Simplicity and functionality are the guiding principles for timeless elegance. Experiments with unusual design were tried, but these were relatively rare. Rather, the firm's designs for the case, dial, hands, and especially its signature crown adhered to the "form-follows-function" modernist tradition.

Machine Age Beauty

This ladies' wristwatch combines classical elements with a Machine Age aesthetic. Concealed within the elaborate wristband is a small watch.

Patek, Philippe & Cie, S.A.
Geneva, 1945 (movement), 1944 (case)
Reference 2126, Caliber 8-80 baguette,
Movement No. 842 390
W. 28 mm; P-1428

Early Reverso

The "Reverso" case of this men's wristwatch allows the wearer to flip the dial towards the wrist, thus protecting the glass. The back bears a dedication from Charles and Jean Stern: "Souvenir of 20 years of collaboration, 1913–1933, your friends Charles and Jean." Designed after the ideas of César de Trey (1876–1935) and Jacques-David LeCoultre (1875–1948) in 1931, only eight cases of the Reverso type were sold.

Patek, Philippe & Cie,
Société Anonyme
Geneva, 1929 (movement), 1932 (case)
Reference 106, Caliber 9''',
Movement No. 822 399
W. 23 mm; P-575

Eiffel Tower	Manta Ray	Twisted Elegance

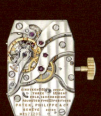		

Collectors named this men's wristwatch "The Eiffel Tower" because the shape of the lugs resembles the pillars at the base of the famous Paris monument.

Patek, Philippe & Cie, S.A.
Geneva, 1948
Reference 2441, Caliber 9-90,
Movement No. 971 205
W. 30 mm; P-1000

The flared sides of this wristwatch designed for men evoke the wings of a manta ray, which became its nickname.

Patek, Philippe & Cie, S.A.
Geneva, 1957 (movement), 1956 (case)
Reference 2554, Caliber 9-90,
Movement No. 977 086
W. 29 mm; P-616

The lopsided shape of this men's wristwatch was the design of the brilliant Gilbert Albert (1930–2019). Though the dial looks crooked, it is actually divided into twelve equal parts by straight lines.

Patek, Philippe & Cie, S.A.
Geneva, 1961
Reference 3424/1, Caliber 8-85,
Movement No. 857 326
W. 28 mm; P-969

Form Follows Function

| 1800 | 1900 | 1980 | 2000 |

Transformation

This oversized men's wristwatch is a fine example of an officier-type watch. The hinged cover and screwed-on lugs are a sign of its origins as a converted pocket watch.

Patek, Philippe & Cie,
Société en nom collectif
Geneva, 1899 (movement), 1918 (case)
Caliber 14''', Movement No. 112 726
Ø 39 mm; P-1321

Staybrite

One of the oldest pieces in Patek Philippe's legendary Calatrava family, this men's wristwatch is equipped with a very early center second hand, a response to the 20th-century's obsession with speed and exact timing. In keeping with this modern functionality, its case is made of a non-corroding steel alloy marketed as "Staybrite."

Patek, Philippe & Cie, Société Anonyme
Geneva, 1919 (movement), 1934 (case)
Reference 96 SC, Caliber 12''',
Movement No. 173 103
Ø 31 mm; P-952

Water Resistance

The water-resistant case of this men's wristwatch houses a Caliber 12-600, Patek Philippe's first self-winding movement. Introduced to the public in 1953 at the Swiss Industries Fair in Basel, reference 2526 proved an instant success.

Patek, Philippe & Cie, S.A.
Geneva, 1954 (movement), 1955 (case)
Reference 2526, Caliber 12-600 AT,
Movement No. 761 531
Ø 36 mm; P-597

Entry to the Crown

The yellow gold watchcase for a ladies' wristwatch can be folded outward to allow access to the crown. The hinge is accented with rubies and diamonds.

Patek, Philippe & Cie, S.A.
Geneva, 1939 (movement), 1940 (case)
Reference 1209, Caliber 4''' baguette,
Movement No. 841 126
W. 16 mm; P-1019

Rows of Diamonds

This ladies' wristwatch on a braided gold cord bracelet conceals the dial under a rounded cover, set with rows of diamonds.

Patek, Philippe & Cie, S.A.
Geneva, 1946 (movement), 1947 (case)
Reference 2243, Caliber 8-80 rectangular, Movement No. 842 637
W. 24 mm; P-1620

Form Follows Function

Seventies Style

This ladies' wristwatch—with matching earrings and ring—is set with 26 diamonds, 18 lapis lazuli, and 18 corals. The flashy color scheme, as well as the shape of the wristwatch, reflects the joyful and exuberant fashions of the 1970s.

Patek, Philippe S.A.
Geneva, 1978 (movement), 1976 (case)
Reference 4406/2J-010, Caliber 16-250,
Movement No. 1 278 982
W. 35 mm; P-1960

Nature in the Raw

Butterfly Wings

This ladies' wristwatch exemplifies the avant-garde look of Patek Philippe watches of the early 1960s. The uneven gold nuggets suggest nature in the raw, yet hidden beneath was a precision watch movement caliber 8-85.

Patek, Philippe & Cie, S.A.
Geneva, 1961 (movement), 1960 (case)
Reference 3295, Caliber 8-85,
Movement No. 857 238
W. 32 mm; P-1392

The harmonious proportions of the Golden Ellipse family of watches made them highly desirable as jewelry. This one came with matching earrings. Its movement was custom-made for jeweled watches. Parts of the bracelet, the dial, and the earrings of the set are made of real butterfly wings.

Patek, Philippe S.A.
Geneva, 1970
Reference 4117/1 "Ellipse," Caliber 13.5-320, Movement No. 1 242 426
W. 25 mm; P-584

Made for the U.S.A.

American Patrons

Patek Philippe always had a special connection with the U.S.A. In November 1854, Antoine Norbert de Patek (1812–1877) traveled to America by steamboat and returned to Geneva in April 1855 with a full order book that would keep the firm busy for a year. At that time, America was the most highly mechanized society in the world. The industrial dynamism of the New World energized Patek in his quest to firmly anchor the company in the U.S. market.

Around eighty years later, in 1937 Henri Stern (1911–2002), representing the company's new owners, headed to New York. He stayed twenty-one years in the city, where he established the Henri Stern Watch Agency. Americans developed a passion for Patek Philippe watches: While on tour, jazz master Duke Ellington (1899–1974) stopped by the company's Salon in Geneva, where he bought a wristwatch with a chronograph (page 67, P-1247). West Berlin Mayor Willy Brandt (1913–1992) presented a Patek Philippe desk clock to John F. Kennedy (1917–1963) in 1963 on the occasion of the president's "Ich bin ein Berliner" speech. Wealthy American industrialists became major patrons. They commissioned the firm to create some of the most advanced watches ever made.

In 1932, the company made for New Jersey railroad investor Henry Graves Jr. (1868–1953) the "Graves Supercomplication"—still the world's most expensive watch. James Ward Packard (1863–1928), manufacturer of luxury automobiles, was in awe of Patek Philippe's pocket watches with special functions; he acquired an astronomical pocket watch (page 65, P-704).

For Graves and Packard, the watches made by Patek Philippe were the embodiment of progress. The Swiss company was at the top of its game. Today it still maintains its headquarters in New York's Rockefeller Center, a modernist jewel. During the Depression, Europeans criticized Americans for selling their souls to the machine. But Patek Philippe showed that a beautifully conceived mechanism—the perfect watch—could lift the human spirit, helping it through even the most difficult times.

Packard's Night Sky

This "astronomical" pocket watch was one of many watches made specifically for American automobile manufacturer James Ward Packard (1863–1928). Known today simply as the "Packard," it has ten complications and was the first Patek Philippe watch to include a map of the night sky, this one set to the latitude of Packard's hometown of Warren, Ohio. Rotating once every 24 hours, the miniature sky chart replicates the daily motions of the celestial sphere.

Patek, Philippe & Cie,
Société Anonyme
Geneva, 1925 (movement), 1926 (case)
Caliber 19''', Movement No. 198 023
Ø 55 mm; P-704

Made for the U.S.A.

200 %

Graves' Complication

It took seven years for Patek Philippe to produce this pocket watch, known as a Grand Complication—a watch with 12 complications—for the renowned watch collector Henry Graves Jr. (1868–1953).

Patek, Philippe & Cie,
Société Anonyme
Geneva, 1919 (movement), 1921 (case)
Caliber 20''', Movement No. 174 961
Ø 62 mm; P-1497

Teetor's Repeater

Delivered in 1924 to Ralph R. Teetor (1890–1982), the American automotive engineer who later invented cruise control, this is Patek Philippe's first wristwatch with a minute repeater. Blind since childhood, Teetor wanted a watch that allowed him to hear the exact time.

Patek, Philippe & Cie,
Société Anonyme
Geneva, 1901 (movement), 1924 (case)
Caliber 10''', Movement No. 112 057
W. 30 mm; P-1157

Duke Ellington's 1563

While touring Europe in 1948, jazz master Duke Ellington (1899–1974) bought this waterproof wristwatch with split-seconds chronograph at Patek Philippe in Geneva. Keeping time accurately was of course highly valued by jazz musicians.

Patek, Philippe & Cie,
Société Anonyme
Geneva, 1946
Reference 1563, Caliber 13-130 R,
Movement No. 863 791
Ø 35 mm; P-1247

67

Every Second Counts

1862   1900   2000

Inventing the Chronograph

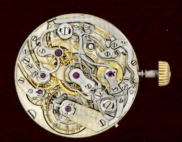

The chronograph measures and records the duration of an event. "Chronograph" comes from the Greek and literally means "time writer." The first chronographs recorded, or "wrote," measurements on the watch dial with a small drop of ink (page 70, P-509).

Watches that measure only the duration of an event are called stopwatches, whereas "chronographs" refer to watches with the usual indications of hour, minute, and second that perform the additional function of a stopwatch.

Chronographs first appeared in an 1821 French patent. But forerunners go back to the 18th century. In 1902, Patek Philippe patented a double chronograph, also called the "rattrapante chronograph" or "split-seconds chronograph." Thanks to its dual second hands, multiple events can be individually "stopped," such as when horses in a race reach the finish line. The aforementioned patent describes the mechanism of a pocket watch, but in 1923 Patek Philippe, in its quest for the "perfect watch," became the first company to integrate a double chronograph into a wristwatch—a remarkable feat in the miniaturization of movements (page 69, P-1505).

The tachymeter, added to chronographs in the 1920s, could calculate the speed of an event. In our modern world of "faster, higher, and farther," speed is the measure of all things. Able to track speeds far beyond real-world experience, tachymeter scales of up to 1,000 kilometers per hour conjured intoxicating visions of a future in which technology knows no limits. Fueling these visions was the fascination with the speed of light in Einstein's theory of relativity, the invention of modern rockets, and other futuristic developments. These were popularized by science fiction writers, but also enshrined on artists' canvases, in the films of movie makers, the eerie sounds of electronic music pioneers, and in the buildings of modern architects.

With the chronograph wristwatch, Patek Philippe joined this march into the future as it continued on the path toward a universal wristwatch that could do almost anything one could wish for.

Split Seconds

Of the officier type, this is the first wristwatch to be equipped with a split-seconds chronograph. Set into motion by a button in the crown, the hands can measure any number of events. The knob between 1 and 2 o'clock controls the movement of the hands. Useful in sports events, the watch was sold in 1923 to the president of the Juventus soccer club in Turin, Italy. Originally it was a pocket watch, as indiated by the hinged back and screwed lugs.

Patek, Philippe & Cie,
Société Anonyme
Geneva, 1903 (movement), 1923 (case)
Caliber 12¼''' extra-flat,
Movement No. 124 824
Ø 33 mm; P-1505

Every Second Counts

1800   1862   1900   2000

150 %

A Drop of Ink

Pulsometer

When a button on the winding crown is pushed on this inking chronograph, the hand drops a dot of ink on the dial. The hand rotates once per minute, with a fifth of a second being the smallest time interval that can be read. Before the next measurement, the ink must be wiped off the dial with a small cloth.

Patek, Philippe & Cie,
Société en nom collectif
Geneva, 1891 (movement), 1894 (case)
Caliber 20''', Movement No. 86 908
Ø 56 mm; P-509

The dial of this wrist chronograph with pulsometer for medical use indicates that the scale is calibrated for five respirations.

Patek, Philippe & Cie,
Société Anonyme
Geneva, 1948
Reference 1579, Caliber 13-130,
Movement No. 867 402
Ø 36 mm; P-1251

Caliber 13-130

Reference 3971

Tachymeter

The case of this water-resistant chronograph is made of stainless steel. It houses a caliber 13-130, which set the standard for high-end chronographs. The tachymeter scale is graduated for one mile. Since the 1940s, stainless steel or a combination of stainless steel and gold has been used for cases.

Patek, Philippe & Cie, Société Anonyme
Geneva, 1950
Reference 1463, Caliber 13-130,
Movement No. 867 980
Ø 35 mm; P-872

Reference 1436 was the first split-seconds chronograph which went into serial production by Patek Philippe. It was manufactured from 1938 until 1971. A round button on the winding crown activates the mechanism; the tachymeter is calibrated to 1,000 meters.

Patek, Philippe & Cie,
Société Anonyme
Geneva, 1956 (movement), 1962 (case)
Reference 1436, Caliber 13''',
Movement No. 868 990
Ø 33 mm; P-1169

This wristwatch with chronograph, 30-minute register, and perpetual calendar was introduced in 1986.

Patek, Philippe S.A.
Geneva, 1986 (movement), 1985 (case)
Reference 3971, Caliber 27-70 Q,
Movement No. 875 030
Ø 36 mm; P-695

The Quartz Watch

The Stern family, owners of Patek Philippe since 1932, recognized early the limits of the mechanical watch. In 1948, they established an Electronic Division to measure time with quartz rather than a balance. Quartz crystals oscillate several thousand times faster than a mechanical balance. Because accuracy increases with frequency, quartz watches are far more precise. Another advantage of quartz is that jolts to the case almost never disturb the rhythm.

The principles of making a crystal oscillate and capturing its natural frequency as a time standard had been well known since the 1920s. Quartz technology was fully mastered in the 1950s, marking the second time since 1657, when the pendulum and the spiral spring were introduced, that the accuracy of clocks made a huge leap. Accuracy in mechanical watches came at a high price; regulating them could account for almost half the cost of manufacture.

Miniaturization of electronics became possible with the invention of transistors in 1947 and integrated circuits in the 1960s. To keep electronic watches charged, Patek Philippe experimented with solar cells and "accumulators." In 1952, the company made its first fully electronic clock and, in 1956, built the world's first miniaturized quartz chronometer (page 74, PE-24).

Quartz movements with photoelectric cells paved the way towards Patek Philippe's dream of the "perfect watch" that never had to be wound or reset. The company joined forces with other Swiss watch manufacturers to make a quartz movement small enough for a wristwatch, with first results brought to market in 1970. But the Swiss watch industry was plunged into deep crisis by much cheaper Japanese quartz watches. Every Swiss watch company was fighting for its life.

Patek Philippe responded with calm and deliberateness. Then-president Philippe Stern (born 1938) made the bold decision to give up quartz technology and redirect the firm back to its roots in the traditional mechanical watch—a risky but, as it turned out, spectacularly successful strategy.

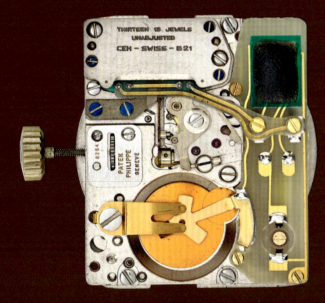

Beta 21

The white gold case of this Ellipse men's wristwatch, reference 3603/1, houses the Beta 21 caliber, developed by the Centre Électronique Horloger in Neuchâtel. The organization was founded in 1962 by the Swiss Watch Industry Association to develop a very precise electronic wristwatch for the mass market.

Patek, Philippe S.A.
Geneva, 1974 (movement), 1973 (case)
Reference 3603/1 "Ellipse," Caliber CEH-Beta 21, Movement No. 8264
W. 33 mm; P-585

250 %

The Heart of the Machine

1800   1900   1948   1985   2000

Triumph of Neptune

This dome clock has a mechanical movement, caliber 17-250, powered by a photoelectric cell in the dome. The cloisonné enamel scenes are after "The Triumph of Neptune" by Nicolas Poussin (1594–1665).

Patek, Philippe S.A.
Geneva, 1971
Reference 776.07, Caliber 17-250,
Movement No. 874 549
H. 215 mm; PE-3

High-Frequency Quartz

Designed by Patek Philippe in 1956, this was the first completely autonomous high-precision electronic quartz clock, and the smallest quartz clock built up to that time. The gray tube houses the high-frequency quartz crystal. It received the United States Miniaturization Award in 1958.

Patek, Philippe & Cie,
Société Anonyme
Geneva, 1956 (movement),
circa 1983 (case)
Prototype
H. 184 mm; PE-24

Solar Powered

This mechanical table clock from 1965 is equipped with a perpetual calendar and powered by a solar cell in the top of the case. Patek Philippe pioneered solar-powered clocks, producing the first of the type in 1952.

Patek, Philippe & Cie,
Société Anonyme
Geneva, 1964 (movement), 1965 (case)
Reference 503/24, Caliber 17-250,
Movement No. 873 556
W. 210 mm; PE-14

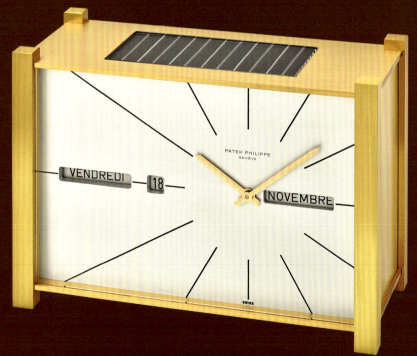

75

Future Meets Past

Enamel Painting Reborn

Even though Patek Philippe was a pioneer of the quartz technology that would revolutionize the watch industry, it kept an eye on traditional craftsmanship. Seventeenth-century Geneva had become the mecca of enamel painting on watch cases. Starting in the late 1960s, Patek Philippe began to revive that brilliant era with a few pieces decorated with the same technique. In the modern high-tech environment, Patek Philippe was swimming against the tide.

The quartz watch was all about speed, mass production, and high accuracy at low cost. In contrast, enameling was an excruciatingly slow process: Sometimes it took a year to paint a small watch case. Indeed, in the workshop of an enameler, time almost seemed to stand still. A moment's inattention could ruin months of work. No wonder experienced enamelers say their education never ends. In lending its name and prestige to this artistic tradition, it was as if Patek Philippe were telling the whole watch industry to slow down and remember where they had come from.

The fast-paced modern world posed a grave threat to Geneva's enameling community, which, along with years of precious, accumulated knowledge, almost died out. Schools of enamel painting began to close their doors. Among the survivors was master teacher Carlo Poluzzi (1899–1978), considered the 20th century's greatest enameler.

In 1967, he extended the life of the tradition by introducing his star pupil, Suzanne Rohr (born 1939), to the president of Patek Philippe, Henri Stern (1911–2002). After their meeting, she went on to work for the company for forty years.

Henri Stern and his son Philippe (born 1938) resolved to keep this Genevan craft alive. At a time when there were very few enamelers left, Patek Philippe almost single-handedly revived the market for this technique. Because of their efforts, the craft of enamel painting not only survives today, but thrives. In many ways, Patek Philippe took a singular position in the watch industry, with one foot in the future and the other in the past.

Suzanne Rohr's enamel miniature on the back of this dress watch is based on Jean-Baptiste Camille Corot's (1796–1875) "Ville-d'Avray." The original painting from around 1865 is today in the National Gallery of Art in Washington, D.C.

Patek, Philippe S.A.
Geneva, 1976 (movement),
1973 (case), 1976 (enamel painting)
Reference 866/69, Caliber 17-170,
Movement No. 932 674
Ø 47 mm; P-258

Rohr's Ville-d'Avray

77

Future Meets Past

| 1800 | 1900 | 1960 | 2000 |

The dial of this men's wristwatch, called "Whaleboat," is crafted in cloisonné enamel. Thin gold wires contain and frame various enamel colors, depicting a three-masted ship.

Patek, Philippe & Cie,
Société Anonyme
Geneva, 1952 (movement), 1951 (case)
Reference 1595, Caliber 12-120,
Movement No. 938 366
Ø 35 mm; P-1330

150 %

Whaleboat

Appropriate to this dress watch, the enamel painting on gold by Suzanne Rohr (born 1939) is after Jean-Honoré Fragonard's (1732–1806) "The Fountain of Love." The original from 1785 is today in the Wallace Collection, London. Engravings after this painting were made shortly after 1785 and contributed greatly to its popularity.

Patek, Philippe S.A.
Geneva, 1973
Reference 866/34, Caliber 17-170,
Movement No. 932 207
Ø 47 mm; P-184

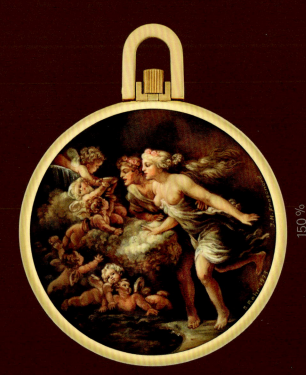

150 %

Fountain of Love

78

Gracing this dress watch, the enamel painting in gold by Marthe Bischoff (1909–1991) is a miniature copy of Jacques-Louis David's (1748–1825) "The First Consul Crossing the Alps at Great Saint Bernard Pass," dated 1800. It was one of the most commonly reproduced images of Napoleon Bonaparte (1769–1821).

Patek, Philippe S.A.
Geneva, 1971 (movement),
1970 (case), 1971 (enamel painting)
Reference 866/03, Caliber 17-170,
Movement No. 931 960
Ø 47 mm; P-176

Napoleon I

This men's wristwatch is named the "Polo," for the polo player depicted on the dial in colorful cloisonné enamel. Indexes are in applied gold dot and baton. The seconds are indicated on a small subdial at 6 o'clock.

Patek, Philippe & Cie,
Société Anonyme
Geneva, 1965 (movement), 1953 (case)
Reference 2471, Caliber 9-90,
Movement No. 977 803
W. 24 mm; P-848

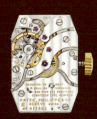 

The Polo

Future Meets Past

The enamel painting on gold by Suzanne Rohr on this dress watch is titled "The Capture of Puerto Bello." It is a copy of a painting by George Chambers Sr., circa 1839, now in the collection of the Royal Museums in Greenwich, U.K.

Patek, Philippe S.A.
Geneva, 1975 (movement),
1973 (case), 1975 (enamel painting)
Reference 866/61, Caliber 17-170,
Movement No. 932 562
Ø 47 mm; P-273

Capture of Puerto Bello

This dress watch is enamel-painted on gold by Suzanne Rohr, after Jean Dubois' (1789–1849) "The Mont Blanc Mountain Range Seen from Pressy." The original painting in gouache, dated 1825, is now in the Musée d'art et d'histoire, Geneva, Switzerland. Dubois, a Genevan artist, is known for his small-frame Swiss landscape paintings, precursors to today's picture postcards for tourists.

Patek, Philippe S.A.
Geneva, 1980 (movement),
1970 (case), 1982 (enamel painting)
Reference 865/54, Caliber 17-170,
Movement No. 933 061
Ø 48 mm; P-514

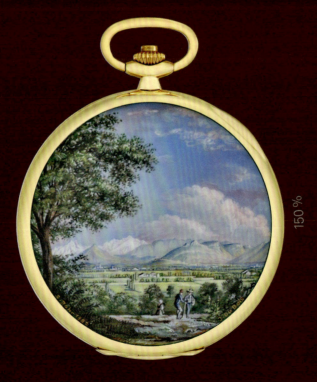

Mont Blanc

Carlo Poluzzi (1899–1978) based his enamel copy on this case-back of a watch on the Frans Hals (c. 1580–1666) painting "Gypsy Girl." It took him almost a year to complete, sometimes using brushes of a single hair. The original painting, dated circa 1625, is in the Louvre, Paris.

Carlo Poluzzi
Geneva, circa 1955
Ø 48 mm; E-50

200 %

"Gypsy Girl"

Enamel-painted by Suzanne Rohr on gold on this dress watch, "San Giorgio Maggiore" is a miniature copy of Francesco Guardi's (1712–1793) original painting, dated circa 1765–1775, today in the State Hermitage Museum in Saint Petersburg, Russia.

Patek, Philippe S.A.
Geneva, 1975
Reference 866/60, Caliber 17-170,
Movement No. 932 563
Ø 47 mm; P-270

San Giorgio Maggiore

81

Modernity and Tradition

1860　　　　　　　　　　　　　　　　　　　　1975　　　　2000

The Lure of Complications

Watches with multiple complications are the glory of watchmaking. Complications are special features that go beyond the usual indications of hours, minutes, and seconds. These finely tuned timekeepers originated in the Swiss Jura, the city of Geneva, and the workshops of Patek Philippe, innovation hot spots where enthusiastic watchmakers competed to fit as many complications as possible into a watch.

The gear trains involved are a unique mixture of the modern and traditional. The makers drew upon the knowledge of their forebears and the inspiration of their peers. Shunning factory work with its typical division-of-labor routine, they operated independently, building the entire watch from A to Z—handcrafting each wheel, lever, and screw, constantly refining their skills. The modernist mantra "less-is-more" is compelling, but these expert watchmakers created breathtaking beauty not from simplicity, but from complex structures in which hundreds of parts blend together as voices in a fugue. Their creations, far from being antiquated, are state-of-the-art testaments to modernity and technological progress.

Complications fall into three general categories: "timing," such as a chronograph; "astronomical," such as a calendar; and "striking," such as a repeater. Watches with two or three complications are called, respectively, "double complications" or "triple complications"; with more than three—indeed some have more than thirty—"Grand Complications." True watch enthusiasts hungered for ever more complications, even as it became difficult to keep track of so many of them. Just the feeling of personally owning such a remarkable device was enough. Imagine the pride in carrying in your pocket or on your wrist a perpetual calendar, effortlessly vaulting leap years with precise accuracy into the far future.

The pocket watches presented in this chapter date from the earliest years of Patek Philippe to the 1970s. Each is a unique piece, either commissioned by a client or made for international expositions. The company used public exhibitions of its acrobatic marvels to convert admirers into passionate collectors.

Stacked Movement

Reference 541, built in two layers, one atop another, has the reputation among watch enthusiasts as the most important wristwatch ever made. Created in 1930, it was the first wristwatch to be equipped with several complications, paving the way for the celebrated "Grand Complications." The movement features a minute repeater on two gongs, a perpetual calendar with a central hand for the date, and apertures for the day of the week, the month, and the phases of the moon. This watch is a one-of-a-kind piece.

Patek, Philippe & Cie,
Société Anonyme
Geneva, 1930 (movement), 1939 (case)
Reference 541, Caliber 11''',
Movement No. 198 340
Ø 30 mm; P-1065

Modernity and Tradition

1800 1860 1975 2000

Triple Complication

This "Triple Complication" is one of the most complicated watches ever produced by Patek Philippe. The pocket watch needs two dials to accommodate so many functions, including a perpetual calendar, moon phases, chronograph, minute repeater, and indications for two different local times. It was presented at the Universal Exhibition in Paris in 1878.

Patek, Philippe & Cie –
Fabricants à Genève
Geneva, 1874 (movement), 1877 (case)
Caliber 19''', Movement No. 47 643
Ø 57 mm; P-153

One of a Kind

This wristwatch with double complication is equipped with a perpetual calendar and moon phases as well as a minute repeater. It was never sold. It is a one-of-a-kind piece, specially for then-president Philippe Stern.

Patek, Philippe & Cie,
Société Anonyme
Geneva, 1964 (movement), 1983 (case)
Reference 3621, Caliber 13''',
Movement No. 866 547
Ø 37 mm; P-710

Versatility

This pocket watch includes a linear perpetual calendar, a double split-seconds chronograph with a 30-minute register, and a minute repeater.

Patek, Philippe & Cie,
Société Anonyme
Geneva, 1931
Caliber 19''', Movement No. 198 434
Ø 51 mm; P-1492

Reference 3974

The perpetual calendar of this self-winding wristwatch has a leap-year indication and a lunar phase. The minute repeater sounds on two gongs. The watch was the first of the 3974 series, launched in 1989 to commemorate Patek Philippe's 150th anniversary.

Patek, Philippe S.A.
Geneva, 1989 (movement), 1988 (case)
Reference 3974, Caliber R 27 Q,
Movement No. 1 906 000
Ø 36 mm; P-745

Time to Listen

1860　　　　　　　　　　　　　　　　1975　　　2000

Grande and Petite Sonneries

Sonnerie watches are feasts for both ears and eyes. Sound was the original way time was announced in Europe, starting with the ringing of bells in towers in town squares. Clocklike mechanisms eventually replaced human bell-ringers. But there was still no visible indicator of the time until after 1350, when faces and hands added to tower clocks became the norm. This marked the real arrival of clocks as we know them.

Clocks with bells also appeared in homes. With a regular chime, they automatically reminded residents of time's passage throughout the day. With watches, this ringing could be a nuisance, and so mechanisms activated only on demand by a button were developed. Patek Philippe was well known for repeater watches that chime on demand, which were especially useful in the dark.

There are several possibilities for signaling time acoustically, "Grandes Sonneries" and "Petites Sonneries" among the most beautiful. Both strike the time on the quarter hour. The "Grande Sonnerie" strikes the elapsed hours before the quarters. The "Petite" version strikes the elapsed hours only on the full hour.

You might think that acoustical timekeepers struck their final hour when electric light bulbs turned night into day in the home and in public spaces, for dials could now be read even at night. But nothing of the sort happened! Ears had become too used to the sound of bells and gongs in portable timepieces. Clocks with repeaters continued to enjoy unshakable popularity as tone sequences became ever more elaborate. The melody of London's Big Ben can even be heard in watches (page 88, P-534).

As if to match the elegance of such sounds, makers of sonnerie watches continued to beautify watch cases. A Westminster chime was even more impressive coming from a watch decorated in the rich colors of champlevé enamel and gold heraldic symbols. With Patek Philippe watches, a gorgeous sound is essential, and the repeater soon became the most sought-after complication.

565 Parts

This pocket watch has both a Grande and Petite Sonnerie, a minute repeater on two gongs, an instantaneous perpetual calendar, indicating date, day of the week, month, and moon phases. Finally, it indicates the leap-year cycle.

This exceptional specimen has 565 components, including 63 wheels and 58 springs. The movement is driven by two barrels and has two gear trains. It is regulated by an anchor escapement and a compensation balance.

Patek, Philippe & Cie, Société Anonyme
Geneva, 1956 (movement), 1964 (case)
Reference 853, Caliber 19''',
Movement No. 861 389
Ø 58 mm; P-343

Time to Listen

1800　　　1860　　　　　　　　　1975　　2000

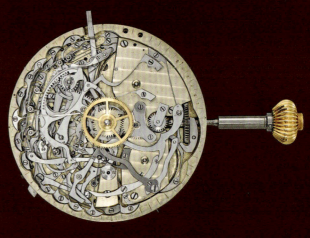

The Duke of Regla Watch

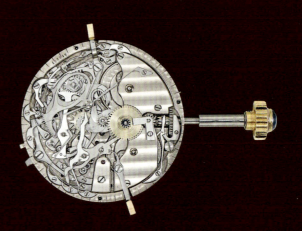

A Watch for Charles XI

 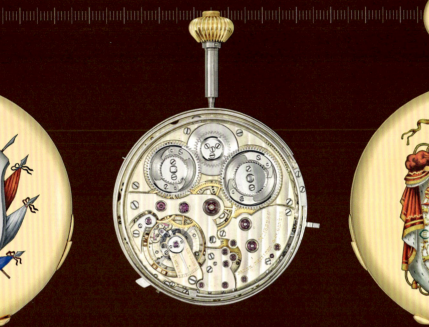 

This minute-repeating pocket watch has a Petite Sonnerie. Probably first owned by the Mexican Duke of Regla, whose coat of arms is shown here, this timepiece produces a unique repertory of sounds, including the famous Westminster chime, trademark sound of London's Big Ben.

Patek, Philippe & Cie, Société Anonyme

Geneva, 1908 (movement), 1909 (case) 1910 (enamel painting)
Caliber 22½''', Movement No. 138 285
Ø 66 mm; P-534

This minute-repeating pocket watch has a Grande and a Petite Sonnerie. It was probably ordered by, or given to, Charles de Bourbon (1848–1909), Duke of Madrid and the eldest of the Capetians. Upon the death of his father in November 1887, the French legitimists considered him king of France, as Charles XI.

Patek, Philippe & Cie, Société en nom collectif

Geneva, 1890/1913 (movement), 1940 (case)
Caliber 19''', Movement No. 174 247
Ø 58 mm; P-1521

Pushing the Limits of the Possible

1800　　　　　1860　　　　　　　　　　　　　　1975　　　　2000

The Grand Complication

Patek Philippe is known for its complex timepieces. The kings of this category are called "Grand Complications," watches that can easily include more than a thousand parts and take up to ten years to develop. They push the limits of the makeable. A mere glance into the movement can make even an expert dizzy.

They contain from three—the minimum—to dozens of complications, including astronomical functions, perpetual calendars, chronographs, and striking mechanisms. The watchmaker's art is to blend these features into a smooth-running movement that fits into a pocket watch or an even smaller wristwatch.

Grand Complications require the mechanical skills of the most experienced and talented craftsmen. By the late 18th century, the "Fabrique genevoise," a system of manufacturing based on division of labor and mass production, was taking hold in the Swiss watch industry. But a group of craftsmen in the Vallée de Joux in the Jura near the city of Geneva thought differently: they resisted the trend toward specialization and standardization.

Fiercely independent, they dreamt of innovating entirely new kinds of watches from start to finish. Their dreams coalesced in the Grand Complication, which soon captured the attention of Patek Philippe. Not only did the company adopt and market the products of these independent-minded geniuses, it carefully nurtured their unique community in the area.

The firm recognized the community for what it was—a hotbed of innovation. The individualistic watchmakers of the Vallée de Joux imagined, designed, and spurred one another to ever higher levels of achievement.

For Patek Philippe, the Vallée de Joux represented a critical resource of knowledge and skill. In return, the firm provided the community an economic lifeline and all-important access to world markets. It is deeply invested in keeping these traditional skills alive and at horology's cutting edge, impressively illustrated by the Grand Complication.

Night and Day

This 18-carat gold Grand Complication pocket watch features minute repeating, a split-seconds chronograph, a perpetual calendar with leap-year indication, diurnal and nocturnal hours, and a 60-minute register, and it shows Patek Philippe's watchmakers at their breathtaking best. It provides no less than a dozen highly readable visual indications alone. Looking over the shoulder of a watchmaker working on a Grand Complication such as this is like witnessing an acrobat's highwire act.

Patek, Philippe & Cie,
Société Anonyme
Geneva, 1961 (movement), 1985 (case)
Reference 946, Caliber 16''',
Movement No. 866 514
Ø 51 mm; P-1072

Pushing the Limits of the Possible

1800 1860 1975 2000

Golden Ears

This Grand Complication pocket watch is noted for its acoustical complications. Just two gongs are needed to produce the sound series of its minute repeater. Tuning them is a task for only the very best watchmakers; like expert piano tuners, they have "golden ears." It also boasts a split-seconds chronograph and perpetual calendar.

Patek, Philippe & Cie,
Société Anonyme
Geneva, 1901
Caliber 19''', Movement No. 112 153
Ø 57 mm; P-264

Reference 5013

This Grand Complication self-winding wristwatch has a perpetual calendar with retrograde date and minute repeater. This is the first piece of reference 5013.

Patek, Philippe S.A.
Geneva, 1991
Reference 5013, Caliber R 27 PS QR,
Movement No. 1 908 000
W. 40 mm; P-857

125 %

Reference 5016

Reference 5016 is a manually wound wristwatch with Grand Complication. Its functions include a perpetual calendar with lunar phases and retrograde date, a minute repeater, and a tourbillon. This watch is the first piece of the series, which was produced until 2010.

Patek, Philippe S.A.
Geneva, 1994
Reference 5016, Caliber R TO 27 PS QR,
Movement No. 1 905 000
Ø 36 mm; P-939

Reference 5004

A special feature of this manually wound Grand Complication wristwatch is the combination of a split-seconds chronograph function, a perpetual calendar with lunar phase and leap-year indication, and a 24-hour-indication. This reference was produced in very few exemplars from 1994 to 2009.

Patek, Philippe S.A.
Geneva, 1998
Reference 5004, Caliber CHR 27-70 Q,
Movement No. 3 275 414
Ø 37 mm; P-1766

Reference 5059

This self-winding wristwatch with Grand Complication incorporates a perpetual calendar with retrograde date, lunar phase, and leap-year indication. The case is made of platinum.

Patek, Philippe S.A.
Geneva, 1999
Reference 5059, Caliber 324 S QR,
Movement No. 3 410 181
Ø 36 mm; P-1787

Family Ties

1900　　　　　　　　　　　　　　　　1985

Fine-Tuning the Brand

"You never actually own a Patek Philippe. You merely look after it for the next generation." This has been one of the company's most popular taglines for more than twenty years; it has been one of the most frequently used phrases in advertising since the 1980s. Everyone seems to know it. And it is usually accompanied by heartwarming images of a proud watch owner handing down a treasured timepiece to a child or grandchild. The message is one of permanence and timelessness, reinforcing the company's desire to be seen as the intermediary between past and future. If the watch has a perpetual calendar, the message is stronger still: Over family generations, a "perfect watch" is forever, and never has to be reset.

Family imagery was a powerful theme for Patek Philippe, binding a family's identity to its watches. Thus, in the 1980s, the concept of watch "families" was introduced. All watches belonging to a particular family share common stylistic elements despite their independent references. Watch family names have unpredictable origins.

The "Gondolo" family, for instance, originated in a successful business relationship between Patek Philippe and a Brazilian jeweler by that name.

The "Nautilus" family, waterproof watches with dials shaped like portholes, shares its name with the famous submarine in Jules Verne's science fiction classic "Twenty Thousand Leagues under the Sea," published in 1870. In the 1970s, the Swiss watch designer Gérald Charles Genta (1931–2011) created the Nautilus with some special features: the porthole design of the case, polished and satin-finished surfaces, and the integrated stainless steel bracelet. Patek Philippe went public with the Nautilus at the Basel fair in 1976. It turned into a best seller and ever since has remained an icon among watches.

The first and oldest watch family, the "Calatrava," derives from the Calatrava Cross, which Patek Philippe had adopted as its brand-symbol in 1887.

One of its younger watch families, the "Twenty~4," refers to the relentless 24/7 pace and constant change of modern life. Accordingly, ads for this watch asked: "Who will you be in the next twenty-four hours?"

A watch family is a living concept that can evolve over decades, always oriented toward the future. Yet, in hindsight, one can discern design and fashion trends of yesteryear. The "family concept" facilitates the identity of a collection as well as communication links within the company and with its worldwide family of customers.

"They work as well with a wet suit as they do with a dinner suit."

Nautilus

The first Nautilus, built in 1976, introduced the concept of the luxury sports watch, a self-winding wristwatch for men. While most Nautilus watch cases were made of stainless steel like this model, a few pieces were made in gold or in combinations of gold and steel.

Patek, Philippe S.A.
Geneva, 1978 (movement), 1979 (case)
Reference 3700/1 "Nautilus,"
Caliber 28-255 C,
Movement No. 1 306 810
W. 43 mm; P-1557

Family Ties

1800　　　　　　　　　　1900　　　　　　　　　　1985

Calatrava

Golden Ellipse

The Non-Watch

This men's wristwatch reference 96 exemplifies the timeless simplicity of the Calatrava watch family. Reference 96 was put into production in 1932 and continued with very few changes until the 1970s. Its successor in the 1980s became reference 3796. Calatrava is Patek Philippe's oldest watch family.

Patek, Philippe & Cie,
Société Anonyme
Geneva, 1946
Reference 96 "Calatrava,"
Caliber 12-120, Movement No. 928 881
Ø 30 mm; P-410

This Golden Ellipse model for ladies is decorated with precious stones and equipped with manual winding. Blue gold, the material of the dial, was produced by a complex process developed in Patek Philippe's laboratories in the early 1960s. The alloy of cobalt and 24-carat gold can only be applied by a special technique. No one had ever seen blue gold before, the main reason for the watch's attraction.

Patek, Philippe S.A.
Geneva, 1973
Reference 3546 "Ellipse,"
Caliber 23-300,
Movement No. 1 222 874
W. 27 mm; P-901

When the Golden Ellipse wristwatch for men was launched in 1968, its shape and blue gold dial were so unusual that it was advertised as the "non-watch." The design immediately became a symbol of international chic, celebrated on the wrist of a lady.

Patek, Philippe S.A.
Geneva, 1994
Reference 4834 "Ellipse,"
Caliber E 15,
Movement No. 1 626 523
W. 26 mm; P-1985

Aquanaut

Gondolo

Twenty~4

Launched in 1997, the "Aquanaut" is the lighter successor to the Nautilus. A wristwatch for men, it is available in several colors. For the first time synthetic materials were used for the bracelet. The high-quality polymer was developed in-house by Patek Philippe.

Patek, Philippe S.A.
Geneva, 2000 (movement), 1996 (case)
Reference 5060 "Aquanaut,"
Caliber 330 SC,
Movement No. 3 023 300
W. 38 mm (with crown); P-1188

The name of the Gondolo watch family originated in the firm's historical relationship with the Rio de Janeiro retailer "Gondolo & Labouriau," which lasted from 1872 until the early 1930s. Introduced in 1993, the Gondolo watch family echoes designs from the 1920s. This watch was designed for men.

Patek, Philippe S.A.
Geneva, 2005
Reference 5014 "Gondolo,"
Caliber 215 PS,
Movement No. 1 891 706
W. 30 mm; P-1771

Launched in 1999, the Twenty~4 is the company's youngest watch family and Patek Philippe's first major release of a wristwatch designed specifically for ladies. As the name promotes, it can be worn for any occasion at any time of day. It focuses less on the product itself than on the customer: the active modern woman who enjoys the freedom to organize her life around her needs.

Patek, Philippe S.A.
Geneva, 2013
Reference 4910/20 "Twenty~4,"
Caliber E 15, Movement No. 5 686 141
W. 25 mm; P-1995

Milestones

1800   1900   1989   2020

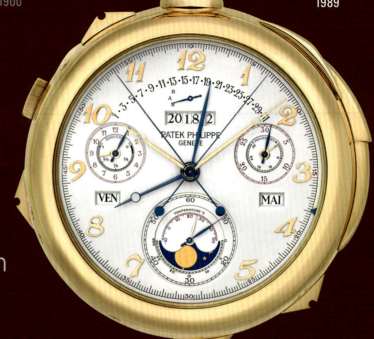

Tradition and Innovation

While always looking to the future, Patek Philippe has been respectful of its history and equally interested in looking back. It regularly celebrates company milestones: its 150th anniversary in 1989, the move to its new building at Plan-les-Ouates in 1996, and its 175th anniversary in 2014. Not just self-congratulatory or marketing events, these celebrations reflect a belief that today's innovators stand on the shoulders of predecessors. Past and future, tradition and innovation are inextricably linked. According to a Patek Philippe slogan from the 1980s, "If you want to know the future, you have only to reach into the past."

For such events, besides the usual souvenirs, the company produces commemorative timepieces in limited editions based on classic watches. These are not just clones of famous old timepieces. Rather, historic references are reimagined and updated with contemporary designs and the latest technology, resulting in some of the most sophisticated devices the company has ever produced.

Brand new pieces were also constructed for such events, but all represent a step forward in Patek Philippe's honored tradition of technological excellence. Illustrative of this practice are three masterpieces: the Calibre 89 marking the company's 150th anniversary in 1989, the Star Caliber 2000 celebrating the new Millennium, and the Grandmaster Chime honoring the 175th anniversary of Patek Philippe in 2014. Fewer than ten pieces of each were put up for sale. But in making them, the company tested new technical solutions, new complications, and new materials in order to improve their regular product lines. Their makers used 21st-century tools, while applying skills based on centuries of horological heritage.

One hundred seventy-five years after Patek Philippe's founding, the company continues to realize Antoine Norbert de Patek's and Jean Adrien Philippe's vision of making the world's best, most complicated, most elegant watches.

Collectively these watches represent thousands of separate parts and more complications than the world has ever seen in wristwatches: perpetual calendar, date of Easter, sunset and sunrise, sky charts, split-second chronograph, repeaters. By some alchemy, they coalesce into a continuous whole, a perfect synthesis of art and machine. Indeed, the past, present, and future merge as well. With these brilliant concept watches, Patek Philippe has proven that tradition is not the opposite of innovation; for innovation depends on inspiration, a rich source to draw upon. And the company found that source in its own heritage. The beauty of a watch can only come from deep within, from the mechanism itself, and, ultimately, from the very heart and soul of Patek Philippe.

Calibre 89

This prototype of the Calibre 89 was created to celebrate Patek Philippe's 150th anniversary in 1989. Only four watches were made after the prototype. Its astronomical complications go back to pocket watches from the 1920s. All told, it has 33 complications made up of 1,728 parts. At that time, it was considered the most complicated watch in the world. Calibre 89 sent a strong message that the company had secured its future with the mechanical watch.

Patek, Philippe S.A.
Geneva, 1980–1989
Caliber 32''', Prototype
Ø 88 mm; P-1989

Milestones

1800 1900 1989 2020

Star Caliber 2000

The Star Caliber 2000, produced for the turn of the Millennium, was modeled on watches Patek Philippe built in the 1920s for the American collectors James Ward Packard and Henry Graves Jr. The back of the case of this oversized pocket watch has a spectacular star chart, with three superposed systems driving the rotation of the star chart, the moon, and the moon phases.

Only five sets, of four watches each, were produced. In each set there is a model in platinum, yellow gold, rose gold, and white gold. Identical except in the design and material of their cases, the watches have 21 complications and consist of 1,118 parts. The Star Caliber 2000 ranks among the most complicated timepieces ever made by Patek Philippe.

Patek, Philippe S.A.
Geneva, 2000
Reference 990/7 platinum,
Movement No. 3 200 021
Ø 73 mm; P-1736

Milestones

1800   1900   1989   2020

Grandmaster Chime

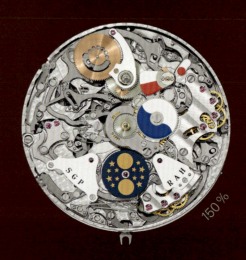

Created for Patek Philippe's 175th anniversary in 2014, the Grandmaster Chime is still the most complicated wristwatch ever produced by the company. Its magnificent filigreed metalwork is matched by the virtuosity of its 20 complications, registering on two co-equal dials, one of which is devoted chiefly to a perpetual calendar.

Time is expressed both visually and acoustically. Audible functions include a minute repeater and an alarm clock that triggers the complete tone sequence for the time to which it is set— a totally novel wristwatch complication. The date is also announced acoustically, one of many newly patented functions on the Grandmaster Chime.

Patek Philippe SA
Geneva, 2014
Reference 5175,
Caliber GS AL 36-750 QIS FUS IRM
Ø 47 mm, T. 16.1 mm; P-1742

2022

PATEK PHILIPPE MUSEUM

Treasures from The Antique Collection
The Emergence of the Watch

1500   1600   1700   1800   1900

teNeues

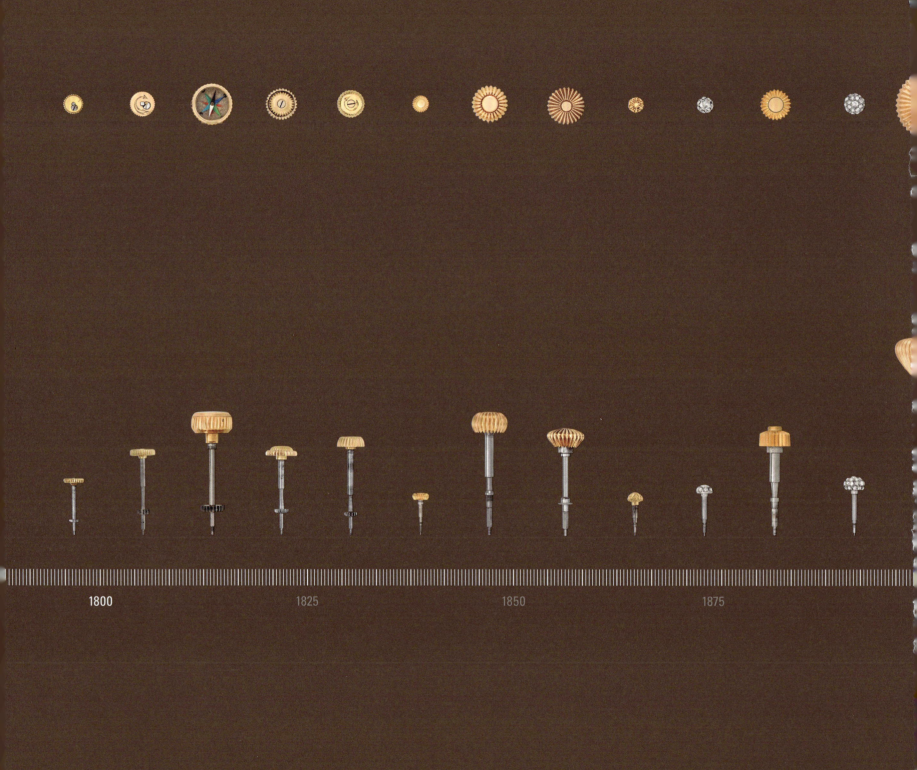

1800 1825 1850 1875